THE REFERENCE SHELF   VOLUME 42 NUMBER 2

THE OUTLOOK FOR WESTERN EUROPE

EDITED BY
IRWIN ISENBERG

THE H. W. WILSON COMPANY
NEW YORK   1970

THE REFERENCE SHELF

The books in this series contain reprints of articles, excerpts from books, and addresses on current issues and social trends in the United States and other countries. There are six separately bound numbers in each volume, all of which are generally published in the same calendar year. One number is a collection of recent speeches; each of the others is devoted to a single subject and gives background information and discussion from various points of view, concluding with a comprehensive bibliography.

Subscribers to the current volume receive the books as issued. The subscription rate is $17 in the United States and Canada ($20 foreign) for a volume of six numbers. Single numbers are $4 each in the United States and Canada ($4.50 foreign).

THE OUTLOOK FOR WESTERN EUROPE

Copyright © 1970
By The H. W. Wilson Company

International Standard Book Number 0-8242-0410-7

Library of Congress Catalog Card Number 79-95635

PRINTED IN THE UNITED STATES OF AMERICA

PREFACE

As the 1970s begin, the outlook for Western Europe is complicated by a host of major questions and uncertainties. Although it is perilous to predict what changes will occur or what the shape of the future will be, it is nevertheless useful to discuss recent developments so as to appreciate the factors and forces behind the events which are shaping the new Europe.

This is likely to be a far different Europe from the one which existed in the 1960s. In fact, every decade since the end of World War II has produced startling and unexpected changes. After the war ended in 1945, Western Europe was primarily concerned with the threat of communism. The threat came both from internal Communist parties, particularly in France and Italy, and from the Soviet Union, whose troops had liberated Eastern Europe from German occupation and then stayed on to play a major role in the installation in those countries of Communist regimes loyal to Moscow. The Western response was the formation of a military alliance, the North Atlantic Treaty Organization (NATO). The dominant member of NATO in terms of military power and economic strength was the United States.

In the late 1940s and early 1950s, Western Europe also turned to reconstruction to repair the ravages of the war. Sparked by massive amounts of U.S. assistance under the Marshall Plan, Western Europe quickly recovered and began a period of unprecedented economic growth. During this time, many of the leaders of Western Europe began to think in terms of economic and political union. This was expressed through a number of treaties which pledged the nations of Western Europe to cooperate in specific fields. Finally, the Treaty of Rome, which established the European Economic Community (or Common Market), composed of France,

Italy, West Germany, Belgium, the Netherlands, and Luxembourg, envisioned a comprehensive economic union. It was hoped that eventually this union would be able to deal as an equal with the Soviet Union and the United States.

However, French President Charles de Gaulle, who came into power in 1958, was not an advocate of supranational union. Though France continued to cooperate with its Common Market partners, de Gaulle resisted any move which would lessen French sovereignty or which would move Europe toward any form of political union. De Gaulle was also opposed to the entry of Britain into the Common Market. He said that Britain, with its special ties to the United States and to the British Commonwealth of Nations, was not truly a European country. Moreover, de Gaulle was eager to lessen American influence in Europe and thus end the hopes of those who foresaw a transatlantic union between the United States and the Common Market countries.

In the 1960s, even as Europe prospered and the Common Market, despite the feelings of de Gaulle and others, continued to forge ties among the nations of Western Europe, other questions arose. In 1961 a wall was built in Berlin to separate the Soviet-occupied part of the city from the Western zones. This wall was built to stop the flood of refugees from Communist East Germany. In the subsequent years, West Germany, a staunch supporter of NATO and the Common Market, began to look eastward and search for means of unifying the country, which has been divided since World War II. The countries of Eastern Europe, long prevented from having too close a contact with the West, were able to shift their policies and think of increased trade and political and cultural relations with the West.

As a result of this changed political climate, the fears Western Europe had of the Soviet Union and of an expanding Communist land mass slowly lessened. Furthermore, the Soviet Union had to contend with growing problems from Communist China and this resulted in reduced pressure westward.

Thus, NATO no longer seemed so necessary as it had once been and it began to search for a new role. After the Soviet intervention in 1968 to prevent Czechoslovakia from liberalizing its regime, Western leaders had to think again about the relevance of NATO and some pointed to the Soviet action as proof that NATO was as necessary as ever. In 1969, after de Gaulle resigned from the presidency, Western Europe had a chance to take a new look at itself to see where it was headed and how far it wanted to or could proceed with the original concept of a European community.

Now, in 1970, basic issues remain to be resolved. Will the Common Market regain its vigor or has the movement toward unity run its course? What will happen to NATO, which some think has outlived its usefulness and which others maintain is still a necessary arm of Western policy? Can there be a solution to the problem of a divided Germany?

This book cannot answer such questions, but it can set the background and explore the alternatives in order to clarify some of the important issues which will occupy a large share of the attention of statesmen on both sides of the Atlantic during the early years of this decade.

The editor wishes to thank the authors and publishers who have kindly granted their permission to reprint the articles in this volume.

IRWIN ISENBERG

March 1970

CONTENTS

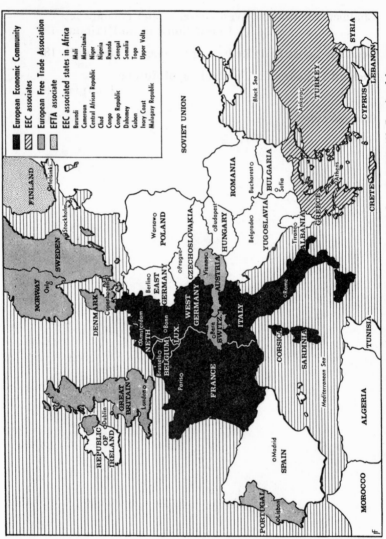

Map by Joan Forbes, staff cartographer. *Christian Science Monitor*. p 1. D. 16, '69. Reprinted by permission from *The Christian Science Monitor*. © 1969 The Christian Science Publishing Society. All rights

European Economic Community

EEC associates

European Free Trade Association

EFTA associate

EEC associated states in Africa

Burundi	Mali
Cameroun	Mauritania
Central African Republic	Niger
Chad	Nigeria
Congo	Rwanda
Congo Republic	Senegal
Dahomey	Somalia
Gabon	Togo
Ivory Coast	Upper Volta
Malagasy Republic	

I. SEARCH FOR UNITY

EDITOR'S INTRODUCTION

For centuries Europe has been plagued by war and destruction as nations fought for territory and power. After World War II, men of vision believed that if a way could be found to unite the countries of Western Europe, then national disputes and differences could be overcome. The creation of the Common Market represented their best hope toward this unity. The architects of the Common Market visualized more than an economic union. Through economics they foresaw a gradual political unification which would result in the abolition of old enmities.

For some years the Common Market moved Western Europe briskly along the road toward economic integration. But its achievements in the political field were slim. Although French President de Gaulle was the most prominent opponent of political union, he was by no means alone in his refusal to support fully the aims of the Common Market. Even in the economic sphere there were some who believed that certain Common Market policies were injurious to the economic interests of their own countries.

The first section of this book looks at the movement toward unity and the numerous difficulties it has experienced in the 1960s. The first article spells out some of the basic facts and figures of the Common Market. It stresses the point that while the Common Market countries make up the world's third biggest economy, they nevertheless suffer from serious defects in their managerial talents—defects which, in turn, stem from their educational systems.

The second article examines the economic mechanisms of the Common Market. The author shows why it is so difficult to maintain a common agricultural policy. Beyond this,

he examines the politics of European unity and states that
the idea of a politically united Western Europe has lost its
relevance. The next article reexamines the Common Market
problems in terms of future prospects. The subsequent piece
notes that the old vision of European unity has become a
caricature and that it is time for Western Europe to think
of ways and means to lower the barriers between itself and
Eastern Europe.

The last three articles in the section offer an outline for
the future. The first of these notes that the Scandanavian
countries are thinking of a union of their own. The following article details the views of a member of the British
Parliament on widening European cooperation. He writes
of a European political community with its own parliament.
The final selection outlines a blueprint for the increased
unity of Western Europe.

WESTERN EUROPE AT SIXES AND SEVENS [1]

The EEC [European Economic Community, also known
as the Common Market, the Six, or the Inner Six, composed
of France, Italy, West Germany, Belgium, the Netherlands,
and Luxembourg] is the world's third biggest economy, with
an estimated gross national product (GNP) of over $350
billion in 1968, and it is far and away the biggest trader. . . .
[In July 1968] after a decade of phased tariff cuts, the Six
celebrated the abolition of *all* tariffs among them—a full
customs union—and the beginning of their common external
tariff. Olivetti typewriters, Renault autos, Telefunken radios,
Dutch cheese and Belgian endive, Bordeaux wine and Bavarian beer can now all compete in a tariff-free multilingual
market of 184 million consumers.

Of their total trade ($111 billion in 1967), nearly a quar-
ter is among themselves; about a sixth, with the European
Free Trade Association (EFTA) countries [also known as

[1] From *Great Decisions 1969.* (Fact Sheet no 5) Foreign Policy Association.
345 E. 46th St. New York 10017. '69. p 53-6. Copyright 1969 by the Foreign
Policy Association, Inc. Reprinted by permission.

the Seven and the Outer Seven, composed of Britain, Norway, Sweden, Denmark, Austria, Switzerland and Portugal]; slightly less than a tenth, with the United States. The Six have special trade arrangements with Israel and parts of Africa (mostly former French colonies) , but, as yet, no common policy for their trade with Eastern Europe.

In day-to-day operations, the Commission of the European Communities not only makes policy proposals, it also administers community law relating to agricultural price supports, export subsidies, business competition, nuclear research, steel output—many of the functions performed in the United States by the Interstate Commerce Commission, the Federal Trade Commission, etc.

The Commission's policy proposals must be approved by the vote of the Council of Ministers, the cabinet-level representatives of the six governments. Since 1967, the council has been empowered to pass upon most issues by a weighted majority, but because of French insistence on unanimity, it has thus far done so only on secondary matters. Thereby hangs a tale of stalemate among the Six. Their progress toward federalism and enlarged membership have both been frozen by a resounding *non* from Paris.

To [former French] President de Gaulle, such goals as a community budget, a directly elected community parliament and an independent executive smack of a supranational authority—to which French sovereignty can never be surrendered. He acknowledges that "in many areas, we have the best reasons for associating with others"; certainly France has reaped enormous benefits from the free flow of goods within the EEC. But other goals set forth in the EEC treaty are still awaiting policy decisions by all six sovereign states.

Sometime after 1970 the treaties governing the Common Market, the European Coal and Steel Community and the European Atomic Energy Community (Euratom) are expected to be combined and rewritten into a single treaty. Meanwhile, their merged executive is kept busy with current problems. Both the coal and steel industries now have surplus capacity. France and West Germany have been going it alone in research on advanced types of nuclear power re-actors instead of sharing in joint Euratom efforts. The eco-nomic health of the members is uneven. Italy is booming, France is struggling to recover from the strikes that plagued it . . . [in the spring of 1968].

Still, the club of the Six has irresistible attractions for aspiring new members—who have been knocking in vain at its door.

"Over His Dead Body"

The blunt headline in the prestigious British magazine *The Economist* voiced the prospect to which most Britons are now resigned: getting into the Common Market only after . . . Charles de Gaulle leaves the scene. Repeatedly since early 1963 the general has shut the door in their faces. [See "The Common Market After de Gaulle," below.] France's five partners want Britain in the club. The British decided . . . [in 1961], after much agonizing, that their future lay in Europe. Why are they still locked out?

Some of de Gaulle's reasons reflect economic realities. The pound sterling, still struggling to maintain its special status as a reserve currency, has been floundering feebly amid Britain's chronic balance-of-payments deficits. Much of Brit-ain's foodstuffs is bought cheaply for sterling from its domin-ions under a system of Commonwealth preferences, which would have to be renounced to conform to the EEC's agreed upon (and much higher) agricultural prices. Higher food costs to the British public would inevitably push up wages—and the price of British manufactures to Common Market customers.

The other EEC members (and Britain itself) acknowl-edge these economic difficulties but are confident transitional adjustments can be arranged—once negotiations for Britain's entry into the Common Market get under way. However, the chief reasons for de Gaulle's rejection, according to nearly all observers, are political.

The [former] French president has a keen sense of history, especially of the age-old rivalry between England and France. Obviously Britain, with its imperial traditions and parliamentary genius, its illustrious diplomatic and commercial heritage, would pose a serious challenge to French primacy in the EEC. (De Gaulle's concept of the Six has been called "a barnyard with five hens and one Gallic rooster.") He reminds the British of the "special commitment that they still have in various parts of the world" (i.e. the Commonwealth and other remnants of empire) and of the truism that they are "not continental" because they live on an island.

But what most disturbs de Gaulle is the Anglo-American "special relationship." Admittedly, this probably will not fade as fast as the Union Jack is being furled east of Suez. Yet the British have repeatedly made it clear that, transatlantic friendship notwithstanding, they feel their best interests lie in being a European equal rather than an American appendage. Nevertheless, the General sees Britain as a Trojan horse: allow it innocently into Europe and American influence on the Continent, already much too strong for his liking, would be further reinforced.

Former Foreign Minister Maurice Couve de Murville spelled this out in a closed session of the July 1967 EEC ministerial meeting. Once Britain breached the club's barriers, he said, other European nations would come flooding in until the original Six became more or less identical to the European membership of the Organization for Economic Cooperation and Development (OECD). This large, rich bloc would then tempt non-Europeans (the United States, Japan, Canada) to try to join. The United States, with its superpower leverage, would surely succeed. Thus "our European Economic Community . . . would become a Western Atlantic complex" looking inevitably across the Atlantic for guidance. In fact, added Couve de Murville, the United States is deliberately seeking such an Atlantic economic community, using Britain as its willing accomplice.

Those closest to de Gaulle say he admits privately that the British have no real alternative to joining Europe and that their eventual entry is inevitable—but why hurry?

The Outer Seven

A century ago a group of early Impressionist painters whose works had been refused by the official Paris salon organized their own exhibition of rejects. The *Salon des Refusés,* as they called it, became a success in its own right. Similarly, the EEC outsiders who have organized EFTA are running a successful show—although most members, like the salon outsiders, hope for eventual acceptance by the inner circle.

The original outer seven of EFTA have added Finland as an associate member; Iceland has also applied. Britain accounts for more than half of the club's nearly 100 million population and its aggregate production, but has a relatively minor trading interest in it.

Seven years after its founding in 1960 EFTA abolished nearly all internal tariffs and other restrictions on industrial goods. Internal trade rose by over 9 per cent in 1967. But unlike the Six, the Seven never envisaged a tight economic union with supranational institutions. EFTA remains a loose but convenient mechanism for trade cooperation among nations with mutual but far from identical interests.

Switzerland clings to its uncompromising neutrality. Neutral Austria (with intimate economic ties to West Germany) and neutral Sweden have vainly sought associate status in the EEC. Denmark and Norway sought full membership but were turned down by the Six. Some Britons who are wary of joining the EEC or weary of waiting to get in have been arguing for a North Atlantic Free Trade Area (NAFTA). In such an English-speaking bloc, they say, Britain, Ireland and Canada—and perhaps some continental EFTA members —could flourish under the benevolent dominance of the United States.

While the Six and the Seven mark time on new moves toward integration, some Europeans are sounding the alarm, expressing concern over another kind of American domination that threatens to engulf all of them.

"The American Challenge"

"In fifteen years the third industrial power after the United States and the U.S.S.R. could well be not Europe but American industry in Europe." With this startling opener to his book *The American Challenge,* Jean-Jacques Servan-Schreiber confronts the challenge head on. The international best seller by one of France's most dynamic and articulate magazine publishers pulls no punches: If Western Europe is not to become a U.S. business colony, it must unite politically and integrate economically.

Today, private American investment in European business—through licensing agreements, subsidiaries, mergers or outright purchases—represents over half the European market in a number of key growth industries. (Eighty per cent of Europe's computers, for example, are made by IBM.)

European firms hold their own quite well against American competition in many science-based industries developed before World War II: chemicals, rubber, metallurgy, electricity, textiles. But not in the major technological innovations—based on electronics and advanced physics—of the past fifteen or twenty years. With a few exceptions, such as jet aircraft and nuclear reactors, Europe lags far behind the giant strides taken by U.S. companies.

This is what is popularly called the "technology gap." But many experts, including the science ministers of OECD countries who held a conference on the subject last spring, insist the term is a misnomer. The gap being filled by American industry is not a European lack of technological know-how. It is a lack of management know-how.

A Management Gap

The Western European countries, according to the OECD study, educate ample numbers of scientists and engineers to keep up with the newest technology. In fact they have a higher proportion of trained researchers than we do: 27 out of every 1,000 workers in the EEC; 28, in Britain, compared to 24, in the United States. Nor is the percentage of their GNP [gross national product] invested in nonmilitary scientific research much lower than ours. (Of course, in absolute amounts, the United States spends much more.) Of one hundred or more major technological breakthroughs since World War II—such as in "wonder" drugs, synthetic fibers and detergents, plastics, data processing, new steel-making processes—nearly half originated in Western Europe, less than a third, in the United States.

But invention is one thing, industrial success, another. To exploit the new technology—from transistors to communication satellites—for maximum efficiency at minimum unit cost, huge sums must be concentrated on relatively few large projects. The investments must be administered by aggressive executives who are willing to take risks and who are educated for resourceful decision making in dynamic new industries.

Here, the gap between Western Europe and the United States yawns wide. The latter produces much better managers simply because it educates its population much better. About 41 out of every 100 Americans get at least some college education. Only 8 out of every 100 Europeans do (roughly half the proportion of U.S. Negroes who go to college). The American labor force has a higher percentage of high school graduates; like the managers, whose training tends to be general rather than scientific, they are more receptive to new techniques and ideas.

Closing this gap would require nothing less than a revamping of Europe's educational system, especially at the university level. Still too restrictive to encourage social mobility, the system produces mass literacy and an elite minority. Training in business administration has barely begun. Moreover, Europeans with science or engineering degrees may not find enough good job openings at home—hence the "brain drain" from Europe to America. Britain alone loses over 6,000 technically trained people each year, mostly to U.S. corporations and research institutes. The Common Market countries have been called "the main world importers of discoveries and exporters of brains."

The More Capital, the Less Cost

Many analysts stress that Europe needs more than better management aptitudes (and attitudes) to cope with the American challenge. It also needs to merge some of its industries—the most advanced, capital-intensive sectors—across national lines. Europewide electronics, atomic energy and aerospace corporations could profit from far higher investment and productivity and better withstand American capital and competition.

Europe is of course no novice at big business, and its business gets bigger every day. But the growth and the mergers, if not in association with American companies, are largely local. [See "Europe's Merger Boom Thunders a Lot Louder," in Section II, below.] In everything from cars to computers to aircraft, the trend is toward one or two giant national firms, proudly flaunted as national assets. Yet Italy's Fiat is no General Motors; Holland's Philips is no IBM; France's Sud Aviation is no Boeing. If such companies (as well as smaller ones) were to join forces with one or more of their European competitors, the savings in production costs would be great. Why then don't they?

Some of the reasons are traditional economic ones. Economic philosophy varies from country to country: the French believe in "planning" (government guidance); the West Germans tend more toward laissez-faire. No legal or tax framework exists for international corporate mergers.

"Eurocrats" are convinced these problems could be solved —by, for example, a special EEC corporate charter for firms seeking to operate on a six-nation basis—*if* the political incentive existed. But it does not. The old pride in national self-sufficiency still holds sway. A European firm can, apparently, tolerate the surrender of its autonomy more easily to a friendly overseas colossus than to a long-time rival next door.

Can the Gap Be Closed?

Some Europeans rail against the American invasion (and the American-style supermarkets and drugstores which are "corrupting" Old World culture) with cries of "U.S. go home." Some swallow their pride and take the profitable line of least resistance. But many others agree with Servan-Schreiber in treating it literally as a challenge—a stimulus to Europe's mobilization of its own competitive resources.

The answer, they say, comes back again to some kind of economic union across national borders. This would allow the European countries to coordinate or integrate (and improve) their educational systems, management techniques, labor supplies, capital sources, research programs, tax structures and corporate practices.

THE COMMON MARKET AFTER DE GAULLE [2]

From the beginning, the European Economic Community has lived from crisis to crisis. One ought not, therefore, to conclude, simply because the Community is now confronted by rapidly mounting agricultural surpluses and a serious disequilibrium [which has since been somewhat corrected—Ed.] between the French franc and the German mark, that this resourceful institution is in serious trouble. And conversely, one should not assume that President de Gaulle's retirement will put things right.

[2] From article by Harold van B. Cleveland, author of *The Atlantic Alliance. Foreign Affairs.* 47:697-710. Jl. '69. Reprinted by special permission from *Foreign Affairs,* July 1969. Copyright by the Council on Foreign Relations, Inc., New York.

In recent years the Community's problems have indeed worsened. Basic assumptions previously unquestioned, such as the irreversibility of economic integration, have been overtaken by events. The morale of that formerly optimistic and uniquely creative organization, the Commission, has declined. The "Community spirit" has deteriorated. The "Community method" no longer seems to work. Few qualified observers believe any longer that the ultimate creation of the "single market" or economic union, contemplated by the Rome Treaty [which established the EEC], is a reasonably sure thing.

Certainly, de Gaulle's negative attitude toward the Community and toward its underlying aim of political unification contributed to this state of affairs. But the Community has problems more fundamental than de Gaulle. Conflicts of economic interest among the member governments have sharpened, while the Community's ability to compromise differences and get on with economic unification has diminished. In consequence, economic integration in Western Europe may have reached its high-water mark. Increasing difficulties and, possibly, retrogression are likely.

During its first years, the Community enjoyed economic conditions peculiarly favorable to progress toward the goals set by the Rome Treaty. These were years of rapid, uninterrupted economic expansion in Western Europe. The Community's first task under the Treaty was to create a customs union to eliminate tariffs and other barriers to the international flow of industrial products within the Community and to erect a common external tariff. The expansive economic environment meant that the problem of competitive adjustment to trade liberalization was far less serious than had been anticipated.

A second favorable factor was that the members of the Community all had large overall surpluses in their international payments. This was in the main the result of American military spending in Europe and the massive inflow of U.S. direct investment into the Community (attracted by

the opportunity to exploit a six-country, tariff-free market),
coupled with relatively low interest rates in the United States
and the undervaluation of some European currencies relative to the dollar. With their official reserves of gold and
dollars growing rapidly, it did not much matter whether or
not the members' payments with each other were in balance.

In its early years, therefore, the Six were able to avoid the
thorny problem of monetary integration—the problem of
harmonizing domestic economic policies to minimize payments imbalances within the Community. Earlier it had been
expected that as trade barriers came down, serious payments
problems would arise. . . .

Thus, two major economic obstacles to integration of
industrial markets foreseen when the Rome Treaty was
signed—protectionism and payments problems—failed to
materialize.

Unlike industry, agriculture could not be integrated simply by removing trade barriers. Each of the member governments supported most agricultural prices and resistricted imports to the extent necessary to prevent price supports from
being undermined. The alternatives were, therefore, either
to leave agriculture out of the "single market," or to unify
agricultural markets by creating a common system of price
supports with unified target prices, jointly financed by the
member governments and buttressed by controls on imports
from nonmember countries. The Community boldly chose
the second course.

Setting common support prices proved to be a thorny
problem. The separate support prices in the member countries differed greatly, reflecting gross inequalities in the efficiency of their agricultural sectors. To get agreement on unified prices, it was necessary to set them rather high—well
above the average level prevailing in the Community before
the common agricultural policy, as it came to be known, was
established.

Agreement on the key wheat price, finally achieved in
December 1964 in a marathon session of the Council of Min-

isters, was facilitated by the fact that the Community as a whole was a net importer of the principal agricultural products. Thus, the higher price level could initially be achieved mainly by raising the level of protection against imports from the rest of the world by means of import levies. The levies are so administered as to keep imports from undermining the target prices. If the Community had been initially self-sufficient—worse, if output of major agricultural products had initially exceeded consumption—a larger increase in the members' budgetary outlays for price support would have been required. The problem of sharing the financial burden would have been correspondingly more difficult.

A favorable factor more critical, perhaps, than any of those mentioned was the transformation of France's economic situation, which happily coincided with the coming into effect of the Rome Treaty. During the 1950s, the French economy had made rapid strides in productivity and internal growth, but it had suffered from chronic inflation and serious payments problems. Although the Common Market was primarily a French conception, it appeared at the time the Treaty was signed that France would be unable to participate without extensive resort to escape clauses. The devaluation of the franc in December 1958 and . . . accompanying stabilization measures did just what was needed. Exports surged, the French economy continued to grow satisfactorily despite restrictions on domestic demand, and the franc changed from the weakest currency in Europe to one of the strongest. The structural improvements in French industry in the 1950s began to pay off in a competitive vigor which French industry had hardly known since the nineteenth century. The sudden strengthening of France's balance of payments and competitive position in 1959 made it possible to go wholeheartedly into the Common Market.

But the economic conditions which favored European integration in the early and mid-sixties were, in part, temporary. France's competitive position and balance of payments gradually weakened as wages in France rose faster,

relative to labor productivity, than wages in Germany and
Italy. Germany and Italy have overcome a tendency to inflation and have enjoyed remarkable price and cost stability
in the last two or three years, while wages in France have
continued to move up a good deal faster than labor productivity. The resulting disequilibrium within the Common
Market reached critical proportions last year, because of
massive wage increases in France growing out of the general
strike in May-June 1968.

The emergence of this particular payments disequilibrium within the Community unfortunately coincided with a
deterioration of the general international payments system.
The climate of international monetary ease which helped
the Market through its early years has now given way to a
"tight" international monetary environment, which magni-
fies the problems of countries with payments deficits. The
result is that the currencies of deficit countries are frequently
under speculative pressure. Deficit countries are strongly
tempted to resort to exchange controls and even to import
controls.

This has happened within the Common Market as well
as outside it. . . . [In] November [1968], France reimposed
comprehensive exchange controls, raised border taxes on imports and even imposed certain temporary import quotas—
all of which applied to trade and payments within as well
as outside the Market. The belief that trade and payments
liberalization within the Community had passed the point
of no return (as was frequently asserted in Community circles in the past) was rudely upset.

The Community is now up against the problem of monetary integration. Either the members' fiscal, monetary and
wage policies will somehow have to be harmonized, or exchange rates will have to be readjusted from time to time.
Otherwise, freedom of trade and payments within the Community will be subject to periodic abrogation by trade and
exchange controls. Of these policy alternatives, only the most

difficult—harmonization of domestic economic policies—is consistent with the aim of the Rome Treaty....

The common agricultural policy, too, has run into serious difficulty. Not surprisingly, high prices have stimulated agricultural output and led to large surpluses over and above what can be consumed within the Community. The surpluses must either be dumped on external markets at prices far below the support price or allowed to pile up in storage. The financial cost of the common agricultural policy is skyrocketing. In the 1968-69 fiscal year, the cost of price supports will be $1.8 billion, of which less than half is provided by the proceeds of levies on agricultural imports. The balance is a direct budgetary outlay. If the target prices are not lowered sharply, the cost of price supports could go as high as $8-$9 billion by 1980, as production increasingly outstrips consumption and surpluses pile up. As output rises, agricultural imports from the rest of the world will decline, so that import levies will make a diminishing contribution.

Under the cost-sharing arrangements, each member makes contributions to, and receives reimbursements from, a common fund. The members' contributions are fixed on a proportional basis, under an agreed formula, while each country is entitled to be reimbursed for the expenses of supporting agricultural prices within its own territory. As a result, some countries are net contributors and others net receivers. Germany, for example, is the largest net contributor and France the largest net beneficiary. Germany's total farm output is a good deal smaller than France's; it therefore costs Germany less than France to support prices. Also, Germany is a much larger importer of agricultural products and accordingly contributes more import levies than France to the common fund. As farm output rises and the total cost of price supports grows, such differences in the balance of costs and benefits under the system raise divisive questions, as is now happening.

Take the case of wheat, for example. Germany is the high-cost producer and France the low-cost producer. To

Germans, the question is whether it makes sense to go on
making larger and larger net contributions to France in order
to help maintain unified wheat prices at a level lower than
German farmers want. The German government is therefore
inclined to ask for a ceiling on its contributions. From
France's standpoint, the question is whether it makes sense
to support wheat prices at a level considerably higher than
the French government would like—and which yields rapidly
growing surpluses—unless France can count on a German
financial contribution which increases as France's wheat output grows. France therefore takes the position that joint financial responsibility (on the present basis) and unified
prices stand or fall together.

In short, with the common prices at their present levels
and surpluses growing, the principle of joint financial responsibility gives rise to serious conflicts of interest among
the members. Logically, the way out is to lower the prices
sharply. But the governments have been unable to agree even
to the modest reductions the Commission has proposed.

The conflicts of economic interest among the Six are,
then, sharper than they were. But this does not wholly explain why the Community is in trouble. What also needs to
be explained is why the Community was able to deal crea-
tively with conflict in its earlier years, while now it seems
increasingly unable to do so. The question is essentially
political.

It should be recalled that the Community has always
been considered by its founders and principal supporters as
a *political* enterprise. The building of a customs union and
then an economic union was seen more as a means to the
end of political union than as an economic measure. The
prevailing view in Community circles was that in the process
of creating an economic union, a kind of supranational economic government would arise, which (so it was argued)
would in time acquire functions in the fields of defense and
foreign policy. Whether or not this expectation was realistic,
it was powerfully effective in motivating the Community's

activities in the early years. The commitment of the six governments to the goal of political union (however remote and ill-defined) made it possible to move ahead rapidly, for a time, with economic integration.

Perhaps the customs union could have been accomplished primarily on its economic merits, but this was not true of the common agricultural policy. The economic benefits of this sort of agricultural integration were too uncertain and the conflicts of interest involved too serious, even at the start, for the policy to stand on its economic merits. Much the same may be said of other provisions of the Rome Treaty which go beyond the customs union, such as tax harmonization, common transport policy and the other provisions whose purpose is to harmonize the "conditions of competition" within the Market. Here, too, the economic benefits are marginal. The motivation and justification for the immense effort spent in trying to carry out these provisions of the Treaty have been political.

A "single market" complete in all these respects was deemed essential—not because the Six could not prosper economically within a simple customs union, but because it was assumed that the more thoroughly integrated their economies became, the more likely they would be to move on from economic integration to political union. In sum, the Community's progress beyond the customs union toward the goal of economic union has depended critically on a common commitment to—and a sense of movement toward—European political unity. It is therefore not surprising that progress has slowed down and threatens to go into reverse. For the commitment of the Six to the European idea has been greatly weakened.

The European idea, whose aim was to build a powerful grouping of European nations organized supranationally and able to play a major role on the world stage, has lost much of its relevance. As long as the goal remained remote and largely undefined, it served to unify the Six and to provide a political *raison d'être* for economic unification. But as concrete steps were proposed to give it institutional form, divisive questions were raised—about the external purpose, the membership, and the internal political structure of the "Europe" the Six would create. The Six have been divided on whether or not the external orientation should be "European" or "Atlantic"—whether Europe should be unified in order to be independent of the United States, as de Gaulle always insisted, or whether a unified Europe should remain associated with the United States, as Germany and the others desired.

The Six have also been at odds on the question of supranationality. Moreover, their views were internally contradictory. De Gaulle, whose aim was a "European Europe," ought logically to have favored a tightly organized supranational union, capable of mobilizing the combined economic and technological resources of the members for military purposes. Yet he had nothing but contempt for supranationalism. The members of the Community who gave general support to the idea of a supranational Europe—Italy, Belgium and the Netherlands—rejected the goal of European independence, thereby cutting the ground from under the argument for supranationality. For why trouble to create a European superstate unless full independence and a great-power role are the purpose of unifying?

Indeed, the wholeheartedness of these three governments' support for a supranational Europe has long been doubtful, although this was largely hidden while de Gaulle was there to keep the question from being seriously raised. The German government, which earlier gave some general support to the idea of a supranational Europe, has apparently changed its mind. In their increasing preoccupation with their Eastern problem, Germans are now inclined to see a tightly organized Europe as a hindrance to their freedom of maneuver in the East.

The idea of political union still hangs in the European air as an attractive vision of power and autonomy. But it has ceased to be a strong moving force in European politics and in the work of the Community. Thus the Community is living largely on momentum. Deprived of its unifying political purpose, its efforts to move further down the road to economic union are frustrated by growing conflicts of economic interest. Indeed, there is a real question whether all the ground won can be held.

This conclusion may seem premature, in view of de Gaulle's resignation and indications that his successor may be more "European." Certainly, it is not easy to judge the relative importance of de Gaulle and the other more objective factors which have blocked European unity. The French president's policies undoubtedly helped bring to consciousness, and make respectable, national interests and attitudes inconsistent with the European idea. Nevertheless, other obstacles would probably have been effective—although the outcome would have differed in detail—even if de Gaulle's opposition had been less.

The disagreements and the divisions which have undermined the European idea have not been simply the product of one man's stubborn will. Rather, they reflect the European nations' objective situation. National states which have found themselves adequate to deal with their economic problems without supranationality are reluctant to contemplate the transfer of their economic power to supranational authorities. Former great powers which have again become used to the exercise of independent diplomatic influence have learned again to prize an independent foreign policy. Countries so long protected by the American nuclear umbrella are reluctant to undertake the costs and accept the risks of reaching for the kind of independence which only political union could provide.

It is, then, unrealistic to assume that the change of government in France will make possible a rebirth of the European idea and such a rekindling of the Community spirit as to give the Common Market a major lift on its way to economic union.

The Community's changed political environment, together with its new economic problems, will affect profound-
ly the Market's internal development. But all the Community's activities will not be affected equally. Some depend more
than others on the political impulse. Those achievements
like the customs union which are essentially completed will
be affected least. Those like the common agricultural policy
which require continual readjustment to changing circumstances, and whose economic value is dubious from the
standpoint of some member governments, are likely to run
into increasing difficulty and to be greatly modified.

The twin principles on which the common agricultural
policy rests—unified prices and joint financial responsibility
—are increasingly incompatible, because the high prices lead
to growing surpluses which make the problem of cost-sharing
politically unmanageable. In theory, there are several ways
of preserving the present system.

First, the common prices could be cut drastically. The
rest of the world would applaud, but the large differences in
production costs within the Community make this solution
improbable.

Second, lower common prices might be rendered more
acceptable to the high-cost countries if direct income subsidies were paid to less efficient farmers in lieu of higher prices.
For example, the common wheat price might be reduced to
the level of wheat prices prevailing in France before the
common price was set, and German wheat farmers might be
paid a subsidy out of the common fund to make up their
loss of income. As a permanent arrangement, this expedient
would raise major political difficulties. European governments and agricultural organizations have traditionally preferred price supports to subsidies. Moreover, it would make
the common prices somewhat fictitious. It would raise the
fundamental question whether or not Germany (in our example) might not prefer a system of national wheat price
supports. For what economic purpose is served by maintain-
ing unified wheat support prices, unless those prices are the

effective determinants of farmers' incomes and economic decisions?

Production controls are a third possibility for saving the common agricultural policy. But, except in the case of sugar, production controls have traditionally been opposed by European governments and farm organizations.

Reflections such as these led the Commission to propose in January 1969 a far-reaching program for restructuring European agriculture. The Mansholt Plan, as it is known, calls for accelerating the outflow of labor from agriculture and greatly increasing the efficiency of farm units. The aim is to lay the groundwork for reducing prices and surpluses while at the same time raising farmers' living standards. But the plan, which calls for joint financing, would cost many billions of dollars. It would be years before the plan would make it possible to lower prices and reduce surpluses. For several years at least, its cost would be on top of the cost of price supports. It would also disturb European farmers' traditional ways. The Mansholt Plan, in sum, is a radical attempt to preserve the "single market" in agriculture, but at a political and financial cost which seems to be far in excess of what the governments will be willing to pay.

Finally, changes in exchange rates, which are probable from time to time within the Community, will put further strains on the fabric of agricultural integration. When the main outlines of the common agricultural policy were laid down in the Community's early years, it was tacitly assumed that after the common prices had been set, the relative value of the members' currencies would remain fixed indefinitely. The common prices were accordingly expressed in terms of a common unit of account whose value in terms of the members' currencies was fixed. The effect was to place a considerable obstacle in the way of exchange-rate adjustments. This was thought at the time to be advantageous, since it underlined the need for monetary integration.

If now the German mark is upvalued . . . the German government will probably have to pay a subsidy to German wheat farmers to compensate them for the reduction in the prices they receive (expressed in marks). Similarly, if the French franc is devalued the common wheat price expressed in francs will rise. The French government, to prevent a further unwanted stimulus to production, may therefore have to tax away the farmers' windfall gain from devaluation. Thus changes in exchange rates within the Community will tend to make the common prices increasingly fictitious. [The German mark and the French franc were subsequently re-valued.—Ed.]

The ultimate outcome is likely to be modification or outright abandonment of unified agricultural prices and joint financial responsibility, and a return to separate national systems of support. Agricultural cooperation among the Six, including preferential access to each others' markets, is likely to continue, however—over the objections, no doubt, of competing suppliers such as the United States. It would not be surprising to see the Community's present system give way to a system like that which preceded the unification of prices. In that period, the members had different target prices. Price supports were financed nationally and buttressed by national import levies which applied to imports from other members as well as from the rest of the world. The levies were so administered as to give the members a margin of preference over outside suppliers in each others' markets. . . .

As the Community loses its political momentum and changes internally, its external relations will also change. For example, the question of British membership will assume a different aspect.

A plausible argument can be made that General de Gaulle's retirement, in combination with prospective changes in the Community, make British membership more likely. In its present form, the common agricultural policy is a formidable obstacle to British membership. It would involve large additional foreign-exchange costs for Britain, which sterling could hardly bear. Britain would have to replace a large part of its food imports from North America and

Oceania with higher-priced food from the European continent. Also, Britain would be a large net contributor to the
common agricultural fund—a further burden on the British
balance of payments.

The changes foreseen in the common agricultural policy
would lessen these obstacles. A simple agreement to give
French wheat, Dutch butter and Italian fruits and vegetables
some degree of preferential access to the British market, in
exchange for British membership in the customs union,
would be much easier for Britain to swallow than the present
system. Indeed, the prospective internal changes in the Community suggest that the problem of British participation
might be dealt with in a much simpler way. EFTA and the
Community might be linked in a free-trade area limited to
industrial products. The continental countries would no
doubt ask as a *quid pro quo* agricultural preferences in the
British market.

Britain, it will be recalled, proposed an industrial free-
trade area to the Six in 1956, while the formation of the
Community was under consideration. At that time, the British government was unwilling to consider full membership.
The proposal was resisted on the Continent, not only by de
Gaulle but also by the Commission and the "Europeans,"
because they saw it as a danger to the Community's political
aim. More recently Britain, too, has been unwilling to consider anything but full membership, on the ground that
anything less would imply a second-class status in the political Europe which was expected to follow. But if political
union is no longer a real objective—if the Community becomes in time little more than an industrial customs union—
these continental and British objections may disappear.

Yet the elimination of certain obstacles, not least the
General's personal veto, does not guarantee Britain's entry.
That depends on whether British participation has sufficient
positive support on both sides of the Channel—which is
doubtful.

Both in Britain and on the Continent, much of the original support for British membership was political. Britain hoped to play a major role in the political entity that seemed to be forming. Those on the Continent who favored British membership did so because they believed that without Britain, Europe would be too small to play a world role or because Britain's presence was desired as a counterweight to Germany and France and to insure Europe's democratic character.

But if the prospect of political union has faded, these considerations, too, have lost much of their relevance. On the Continent, strong official support for British membership is largely confined to the Dutch, with some assistance from the Belgian and Italian governments. But this support seems to be mainly a reflection of anxieties raised by Germany's strength, now increased by de Gaulle's departure and France's economic troubles. As such, it can hardly provide common ground between Germany and the other members to welcome Britain in. France's positive political interest in British membership is also hard to see, if the Community is now becoming essentially an economic enterprise.

The economic interest of the Six in British membership is also somewhat doubtful. France, with its balance of payments weakened and its competitive position impaired, is hardly interested in intensified British competition. The persistent weakness of sterling makes Britain a less attractive candidate, since membership raises a presumption, under the Rome Treaty, of mutual financial responsibility.

On Britain's side, too, . . . economic considerations seem likely to weigh against rather than for immediate participation. No doubt British industry would benefit substantially in the longer run from secure access to continental markets and from more competition at home. But with sterling weak, joining a tariff-free market of this size would probably aggravate, for a time at least, the balance-of-payments problem. A government whose monetary reserves are completely mortgaged and which lives perforce from one set of monthly trade figures to the next may have neither the energy nor the heart to take important financial risks for the sake of longer-term gains.

Furthermore, American policy on the question of British membership in the Common Market is also likely to change. As long as the EEC was seen in Washington as the growing point of a European political union, the United States lent strong support to British membership. Three Administrations consistently supported British participation on the ground that it was essential to create the kind of European political entity with which the United States could live comfortably. Americans, like many Britons, considered British participation essential to balance Germany and France, to strengthen democratic institutions on the Continent and to help keep Europe "Atlantic" and "outward looking."

But if there is to be no political union in Europe, this reasoning loses much of its relevance, and the question of British entry becomes for the United States primarily an economic problem. With our competitive position in world markets weakened and our trade balance in trouble, it would be surprising if the United States failed to raise objections to the inclusion of Britain in a preferential trading system which excluded the United States, especially with preferences for agricultural products involved. Given Britain's growing financial dependence on the United States, Washington's objections would probably weigh heavily in London.

Thus, in the matter of British membership as in the Common Market's own development, the weakening of the political *raison d'être,* along with changes in the economic scene, have altered prospects fundamentally. From this perspective, the lifting of de Gaulle's veto on political unification and British membership seems almost incidental.

The prognosis for the Common Market sketched here may seem unduly pessimistic to those who still see the Community as the first step toward a new political order in Europe. Yet if one can divorce one's thinking from this hope, which once fired the imagination of so many Americans and

Europeans, and see the Community as it is today and as it
seems likely to be tomorrow, the outlook is not entirely discouraging. Europe has prospered economically and its trade
has expanded enormously as never before, although the
Community has not developed much beyond a customs
union. Europe has remained secure and democratic without
political union. Problems there are aplenty, but is it un-
reasonable to hope that these blessings can continue, despite
the troubles of the Common Market?

THE COMMON MARKET: BURIAL OR REVIVAL? [3]

"Whenever kings come together," Goethe wrote, "it is
always bad news." This week [in December 1969] the heads
of the six nations of the European Economic Community
hope to prove the poet wrong when they meet in the thir-
teenth century Hall of Knights in The Hague. The . . .
summit meeting could prove of critical importance in determining the future of the Common Market, and indeed of
all Europe. Since the Market was created twelve years ago, it
has not merely lost momentum but has also shown signs of
coming apart.

The business of the "kings"—in reality the president of
France, the chancellor of West Germany and the premiers
of Italy, Belgium, the Netherlands and Luxembourg—is to
determine how badly they want this economic union to en-
dure and what they should do to revive its impetus. There
was a great air of uncertainty over the direction the talks
would take. As he processed credentials for the five hundred
newsmen attracted by the spectacle, one Dutch official wryly
inquired last week: "Is it to be a burial or a revival?"

The man chiefly responsible for the Market's state of disarray will not be at the huge oval table. Charles de Gaulle
saw the EEC as little more than an expediter of French policies and was determined to keep it thoroughly subservient to
the six governments that brought it into being. On two oc-

[3] From article in *Time*. 94:43-4. D. 5, '69. Reprinted by permission from
Time, The Weekly Newsmagazine; Copyright Time Inc. 1969.

casions de Gaulle vetoed British membership. During one
seven-month period, he ordered his ministers to boycott all
meetings of the Six to demonstrate his displeasure over what
he considered supranational power plays by the EEC Commission. De Gaulle became a symbol of obstinacy, but he also
provided a convenient screen for the other members, who
disagreed too about the way in which the Market was being
shaped. Publicly, the five deplored France. Privately, they
occasionally scuttled Market proposals that collided with
their own particular national objectives.

Bureaucrats and Butterbergs

The result is that the Common Market today is still little
more than an imperfect customs union—which is precisely
what France's President Georges Pompidou sneeringly called
it while serving as de Gaulle's premier. Joint policies on
money and transportation have never been worked out. Uniform tax reforms were supposed to be completed by the
beginning of 1970, but Italy and Belgium have airily announced that they will be unable to meet the date.

The most stubborn problem of all is agriculture. Seventeen months ago, a new agricultural policy was introduced
that called for a single six-nation market with uniform prices
for most farm products. Hailed as the Common Market's
finest achievement, the policy has not worked as well in
practice as it did on paper. French devaluation and German
revaluation shook the price structure. Instead of eliminating
marginal farmers, the Six have kept them in business through
a tangled network of supports and tariffs.

The main beneficiaries are the farmers of France, who
chiefly benefit from the artificially high prices set by the
Market. The big losers are the Germans, who agreed to foot
28 per cent of the agricultural bill in return for a wider market for their industrial goods. The result of the subsidies has
been a dizzying upsurge in production and the creation of
mountainous surpluses—including a 425,000-ton *Butterberg*

and 8 million tons of wheat. Merely to store the surplus farm products costs the Six $400,000 a day.

The French are wary of any change in agricultural policy and are determined to take that matter up before anything else. Certainly Pompidou has enough political problems to handle without having to worry about a bigger rebellion among farmers. Consequently, he is anxious to come away from The Hague with a guarantee that the subsidy system for French farmers will be continued. But West Germany is urging that other accommodations be worked out. The summit delegates will probably compromise by extending the present system for one more year while they work out something better.

The Great Federator

After agriculture has been disposed of, the French may then be amenable to discussing the issue that many Eurocrats count as the most important confronting the summiteers: expanding the EEC beyond its present membership. Applications are pending from Britain, Ireland, Denmark and Norway. Of the postulants, Britain is obviously the most important, and sentiment is growing among ordinary Europeans for British admission. A recent *Paris-Match* poll showed 52 per cent of Frenchmen saying yes. Officials at the Quai d'Orsay [the French foreign office] let it be known that the French were going to The Hague "to begin the process of getting Britain into the Common Market."

The British themselves, on the other hand, have begun to have second thoughts. Two weeks ago, a *Times* of London poll found 54 per cent of them opposed to joining the Common Market. Because trade balances have improved and the pound is stronger, Britain has emerged from its slough of economic despond. "We no longer face the challenge of Europe cap in hand," Prime Minister Harold Wilson told a cheering Labour Party meeting. . . . "Europe needs us just as much as, and many would say more than, we need Europe." What worries the Prime Minister and other Britons, for one thing, is that membership would bring an immediate and politically damaging rise in consumer prices. Butter costs 48 cents a pound in England today and eggs 50 cents a dozen; in Paris, butter costs $1.08, eggs 84 cents.

Britain has other reservations about joining a union in which it has sought membership for so long. One is the fear that Britain will be drawn into a political assembly in which ancient forms and traditions will disappear. Actually, the prospect is remote. Political union was the goal toward which Jean Monnet and other Pan-Europeans sought to steer the Common Market more than a decade ago. The threat of the Soviet army perched across nearby borders made planners anxious to achieve union by any means. Today, however, the Russian threat appears to have diminished markedly; so has the possibility of war between old rivals, particularly France and Germany. These new realities have very much lessened the pressures for political confederation.

Bigger than Japan

Political union is plainly a long way off, if attainable at all, but what of a closer economic union? The Soviet threat has been largely replaced by the American economic challenge, and Europe's economy may one day face eclipse unless it works out some response. The most logical response would be a vigorous, creative economic union that really did look beyond the narrow interests of French farmers and Walloon miners. Such a union, with Britain added to the present Six, would mean a Common Market of nearly 240 million people. Japan has managed to become a leading commercial power —and a growing political force—with less than half that many.

[At the EEC meeting in The Hague, the Six agreed to open negotiations in 1970 on British membership and "reaffirmed their agreement on the principle of the enlargement of the Community." British Foreign Secretary Michael Stewart and West German Chancellor Willy Brandt praised the agreement. A previous meeting in Brussels in November 1969 extended the farm subsidy system for at least another

year and recommended further study on the proposed overhaul of the system. See also "Blueprint for Unity in Europe,"
in this section, below.—Ed.]

EUROCRACY AND A NEW VISION [4]

The universally accepted myth of the 1960s was that
Charles de Gaulle was the only roadblock barring the way
to a United States of Europe. Accordingly, when the General
made his abrupt exit from the political scene . . . , European
federalists were elated at the thought that their cherished
goal was at last in sight. Their euphoria, however, did not
last long. For it is now painfully apparent to observers of
European affairs that de Gaulle was merely a convenient
scapegoat for the failures of other European statesmen. . . .

For public consumption, France's five Common Market
partners talk about the urgent necessity of taking up Britain's
application to join the European Economic Community—an
application which de Gaulle vetoed thrice in the past decade.
But in private conversations with high-ranking officials in
several European capitals, I have been told that British Prime
Minister Harold Wilson's European credentials are "dubious" and that London's continuing economic troubles prove
that nothing useful can be done until after the next British
elections when, presumably, Conservative leader Edward
Heath will take over. In Britain itself, many voices are heard
asking whether their country's candidacy is still relevant. A
front-page editorial . . . in London's mass circulation *Daily
Express* explained "Why we must never join the Common
Market." And the Sunday *Times* editorialized: "The Common Market is losing friends fast among politicians of all
parties, among businessmen and [among] ordinary citizens."

Indeed, the vision of European unity has become a caricature of what it was in the era following World War II.
Jean Monnet and a small band of loyal followers gamely

[4] From article by Arnaud de Borchgrave, senior editor. *Newsweek.* 74:56+.
S. 29, '69. Copyright Newsweek, Inc. 1969. Reprinted by permission.

soldier on, but the impulse toward some sort of political integration in Western Europe is dead. Sterile haggling over petty national interests has long since replaced unity of purpose. European politicians have developed a vested interest in present structures, and internecine feuds seem to absorb most of their energies. "Statesmen" are preoccupied with wave after wave of wildcat strikes, usually provoked by long-neglected domestic problems whose solutions lie in the Greater Europe they lack the political courage to create. Young people have become apolitical and disaffected, unable to find an outlet for their aspirations; they look for a new world and all they find are relics of the past. Only a few specialists still pay any attention to what goes on in the "Eurocracy" in Brussels, where the buck is passed from committee to subcommittee in an endless process.

"Even if we all decided to give the highest priority to putting a European on the moon," says one senior Brussels Eurocrat, "we couldn't do it. Apart from our technological limitations, there would be endless discussions in myriad ad hoc committees on the distribution of responsibilities, financial contributions, the nationality of the three astronauts and of the first one chosen to set foot on the moon." Adds an equally gloomy colleague: "If we go on like this, an American will have landed on Mars while we Europeans still argue about how to get Britain into the Common Market."

Drive

Frustrated by the ever-widening technological gap between the Old and the New Worlds and no longer enthused by the old drive to integrate a half dozen West European nations, many Europeans are now devoting their thoughts and energies to a new goal: a lasting political and economic order, based upon a reconciliation between the two halves of ideologically divided Europe.

In many ways, the concept of a true détente is not so wild a dream. Officials in Western European capitals express remarkably little fear of the Soviet Union—once the catalyst of Western integration. To many such officials, the invasion of Czechoslovakia was seen not as a threat to the West but as a rear-guard action by an aging and mediocre Soviet leadership to save a crumbling empire from total collapse. The worsening tension between Moscow and Peking, and the impending negotiations between Moscow and Washington over limiting nuclear arms, have also induced a growing conviction in the minds of European officials that a European war is no longer a likelihood. In short, the European confrontation—which still involves the largest deployment of troops and weaponry the world has ever seen in peacetime—has lost its *raison d'être*.

Fiction

Encouraging though all this may be, there will be no breakthrough toward a lasting reconciliation in Europe until there is formal diplomatic acceptance of Europe's present boundaries—including diplomatic recognition by the West of the Communist regime in East Germany. (Considering that East Germany is now the world's seventh-ranking industrial power, the diplomatic fiction that the East German state does not exist is becoming increasingly untenable.)

The skeptics argue that recognition of the status quo in Europe would represent a signal victory for Moscow. And if done during the tenure of the present Kremlin leadership, it of course would. But many Europeans are thinking of the post-Brezhnev period.

What we say and do now [a Belgian official recently returned from Moscow told me] will be decisive in determining the options of the new Soviet regime. If we act wisely now, instead of digging in our heels and saying nothing has changed or ever will, Russian leaders will eventually conclude that their present system of dominion in Eastern Europe is incapable of establishing normal, decent relations with their neighbors. East German recognition would seem to be a very small price to pay for a new order in Europe.

CHARTING A COURSE FOR THE NORTH [5]

Devaluation of the franc has been a setback for the overall unification of Europe. But, paradoxically, it has improved the chances for what is known as the Nordic Union.

In mid-July, a month before the Pompidou government reduced the value of French currency, the foundations of a Scandinavian Common Market were laid in Copenhagen. Delegates from the foreign ministries of Denmark, Finland, Norway and Sweden then agreed on the terms of a draft treaty which would establish a customs union between these four countries by January 1972.

There was no need for haste, it was said, because in another two years the Scandinavian nations might all be members of the larger European Economic Community, composed of France, Italy, West Germany, Belgium, Holland and Luxembourg.

But French devaluation has blocked the progress of this original Common Market. Elimination of customs barriers has little meaning unless, as in our own Federal union, the currency of the cooperating states is unified, or at least has a stable relationship, one to another.

If the U.S. dollar were suddenly devalued to 90 cents in Pennsylvania alone, the manufacturers of that state would have a temporary pricing advantage in interstate commerce. Similarly the recent French devaluation, of 12.5 per cent, has priced French exports low and thereby caused irritation and complications within the EEC. The Scandinavian people are already closely tied together, by race, geography, history and commerce. They have been united politically in the past and excepting Finland, where Swedish is widely spoken, have only dialectal differences in language.

They have a virtually uniform legal system and similar extensive social welfare systems. A medical degree in one entitles a doctor to practice in any of the other countries.

[5] From article by Felix Morley, contributing columnist, Pulitzer prize-winning journalist. *Nation's Business.* 57:20+. O. '69. Reprinted by permission.

SAS, the famous Scandinavian Air Service, is run coopera-
tively by Denmark, Norway and Sweden. The royal families
of these three constitutional monarchies are closely akin.
Even the five Scandinavian flags are identical in design,
though different in color combinations.

A visit to all these Nordic countries, including Iceland,
convinces me that their federation would be a natural and
generally beneficial development. Since 1953 that goal has
been quietly forwarded by the influential Nordic Council.
Its attainment will be hastened if the EEC is now forced to
mark time.

"Why wait for the rest of Europe?" is the expression one
hears from business leaders in every Scandinavian city. "Why
not go ahead, in a small way, on our own?"

There are arguments pro and con. Favoring Nordic federation, in addition to factors mentioned, is the slogan of our
own formative period: "In union is strength." Taken separately all of these Northern countries are small, exposed and
militarily weak. Sweden, easily the strongest, has fewer than
8 million inhabitants and if one adds all the people of Denmark, Finland, Norway and Iceland the total population is
still only about 21 million, or approximately that of Canada.
This explains why, during World War II, Denmark and
Norway quickly fell prey to Germany, and Finland to Russia.
Yet, under heavy pressures, Sweden was able to preserve neutrality. Under their leadership, say the Swedes, a united
Scandinavia could form a front discouraging attack from
any source.

There is, however, one political hurdle, erected by the
Cold War. Denmark and Norway are members of NATO,
designed as a defense alliance against Russia. Finland has
eight hundred miles of open frontier with the Communist
giant and will certainly take no step that seems offensive to
Moscow. Since nearly 20 per cent of Finland's foreign trade
is now with Russia it would probably be happy to settle for
a neutralized Scandinavia. But the Western-oriented Danes
and Norwegians will not do so without American blessing.

In consequence, lacking a better East-West relationship, which in essence means cordiality between Moscow and Washington, there is little immediate prospect for any real Scandinavian union. Yet the commercial relations between these countries, encouraged by their membership in EFTA (the British-sponsored European Free Trade Association) improve steadily. And their economies are more complementary than one might think at first glance.

While Swedish industry is extraordinarily productive, the same can be said of Danish agriculture, which exports two thirds of the food raised on its fertile farms. There is a natural basis of exchange across the narrow strait that separates the two countries, soon to be strengthened by construction of an international rail and highway bridge.

Similarly, mountainous Norway, with only 3 per cent of its area usable land, finds a market in Denmark for its abundant hydroelectric power. And Finland, no longer dependent on the "green gold" of its forests, is coming to the front in shipbuilding as well as in general architectural design.

The rapidity of business development since the war has caused the familiar problem of overheated economies, most serious in barren Iceland, where the population of 200,000 is dependent on American military occupation for its fictitious prosperity. The economic future of this remote island, which separated from Denmark to become an independent republic in 1944, is admittedly dubious. It has virtually nothing but fish to export and naturally the Icelanders are more anxious than other Scandinavians to be included in a Common Market which might assist them if the flow of American dollars should be cut off.

But there will be no Scandinavian Common Market, political difficulties aside, without reliably stabilized currencies. The difficulties encountered by EEC also apply to these smaller Northern countries. There is need for much closer cooperation between their central banks than has yet been attained.

The Russians do not want this development, except on their own terms, and clearly believe that time is on their side. Modern merchant ships, flying the hammer and sickle flag, are now familiar sights in every Baltic port and at the great Kronstadt naval base there is a formidable armada to give backing to this commerce. . . .

Leningrad, the Russian window on the Baltic, is undeniably an impressive city. The devastation inflicted on it by the German siege has been repaired. The old Czarist palaces and parks are well restored and none can call the people in the crowded streets either ill nourished or poorly clothed. There are few private cars and no attractive shops. But there also are no beggars and no litter in the streets.

Nevertheless, the contrast with the vivacious, sparkling Scandinavian cities, whether Oslo, Helsinki, Stockholm or Copenhagen, is striking. Under private enterprise they maintain a well-distributed prosperity without oppressive atmosphere. The brighter present, and presumably also the bright future, lies on the northern, not the southern, shores of the Baltic.

In that important inland sea the entire southern section is held by Communist countries—Russia, Poland, East Germany. To crisscross its waters is to realize that the future here is both promising and precarious. It could be that the sheer mass and weight of the Communist bloc could in the long run dominate the Baltic, even without any military action.

It is to avert this outcome that so many Scandinavians, a highly civilized and homogeneous people, are urging closer economic and political ties among their countries. The obstacles are many. If they are to be overcome, not only American sympathy, but also understanding of the complex problem, will be essential.

Even if it requires neutrality, the unity sought would surely strengthen free institutions in an area where they have been indigenous for 1,000 years. That is an objective to which the talents of our diplomacy could happily be addressed, not less so because, by contrast with the Mediterranean, the Baltic is for us the forgotten sea.

AIM: WIDENED EUROPEAN COMMUNITY [6]

Our reasons for wanting a united Europe are essentially political. And many of those who created the EEC envisaged that it would have a major political role. But there are major aspects of political union that the existing Community does not touch upon. A means of working towards a common European foreign policy and a common European defense policy and strategy are politically of extreme importance, and common action in these directions would in no way cut across the work of the existing Community. Here is a fairly direct road to political union—albeit with rocks in the path —but a road which is not barred by any right of veto. . . .

In addition to foreign policy and defense, such a political community could also deal with some subjects that are not altogether excluded from the scope of the Treaties of Rome but which the existing Community has been unable to deal with effectively because of the use of the veto and the resulting political weakness of the Community institutions.

One such subject is international monetary policy. Last November [1968] we saw the world monetary system go to the edge of the precipice; and we saw Europe incapable of any joint action to pull it back. We and the members of the EEC would be among those who suffer most if the system collapses, because we are so dependent on world trade. We need a common European policy—and perhaps a European reserve unit—so that we can ensure, with our united strength, at least a minimum of stability in the system. This could be a field for action by a new European political community, while the enlargement and progress of the EEC remain barred. During this period, political community and economic community should of course cooperate in such mat-

[6] From a speech by George Brown, Labour member of the British Parliament, former Foreign Secretary. *Atlantic Community Quarterly.* 7:387-92. Fall '69. Reprinted by permission.

ters as closely as the institutional difficulties of the EEC will allow.

Another subject for consideration is advanced technology. A political community dealing with foreign policy and defense would have to concern itself with arms production. A European arms production board would enable the Community to reap the economies of scale and avoid undue dependence on America. Such a board would exert a powerful influence on aircraft, electronics and other advanced technology industries. There is at least a case to be made that the political community should extend its sphere of activity so as to meet the "American challenge" over the field of advanced technology as a whole. . . .

Intergovernmental talks should immediately be got under way to consider how to establish a European political community, of which Britain and others at present outside the EEC would be members alongside the existing economic community. It would not be intended to replace the EEC. It would not . . . be intended to exclude any member of the EEC. By far the best way ahead would be for Britain and the other applicants to be admitted to the EEC and for it to assume the role of a political community at the same time and with the same membership.

But clearly this best way is not open—as a result of the veto on enlargement of the EEC and the French government's known reluctance to accept common institutions and common policies—and so I think we should go for the establishment of the political community all the same. [At talks in December 1969, EEC members agreed to open negotiations on British membership in 1970 and discuss further enlargement of the membership.—Ed.] A place should be left open for France—and I am convinced that, if other countries show themselves determined to go ahead, the French will not be slow to join in. . . .

But what is vital is that it should be clear that we would go to the talks determined ourselves not to allow others to water down the proposal so that the political community can be paralyzed, as the EEC has been, by an individual government's power of veto. The political community must have an unchallengeably democratic base. It needs a parliament which has effective power over the instruments by which policy is made and executed. It needs a council of ministers which, in the first stages of the community, must obtain its democratic mandate through the national governments, but which must not be hamstrung by a national power of veto. And it needs its executive arm—a commission with stature and authority—which will be controlled by the council and parliament. The institutions will reach their full development only over a transitional period, but from the start they must be strong enough to give the community the power to decide and to act.

And there will be plenty to argue about at the early meetings on how to get this going.

Such a community would make a great impact on the problems of détente towards Eastern Europe, the Middle East and elsewhere, in the face of which Europe is now so helpless. Such a community, having a European political and its own common defense policy, with the Atlantic Alliance, would give Europe the means to respond quickly and realistically to any political or strategic threats from the Soviet Union. It would enable us to play a much more positive role in the defense of our own continent by having much more impact on the thinking of the Western Alliance.

The invasion of Czechoslovakia has reminded us that this is necessary. [See "NATO After the Invasion," in Section IV, below.] But it does not follow that we should foresee only the bleak prospect of a perpetual cold war. On the contrary, a united Europe will remove from the hawks in the Kremlin the prospect of exploiting our divisions and weakness. On this basis of security, a European political community could build a constructive policy of détente with Russia and Eastern Europe, and could make real progress towards dealing with the German problem.

It must be recognized that no good solution to this problem will be possible until Germany is fully integrated as an equal partner into a strong and cohesive European political community. Suspicion of Germany is still too great in Russia and Eastern Europe for the Russians to relax their grip on East Germany so long as there is any chance that this could lead to a reunited and independent German state which would dominate central Europe. But once Germany—and unless one is looking at the distant future, this means in practice the Federal Republic—is a member of an integrated political community, it will become clear that unilateral action by Germany is no longer possible. Nor, with Germany as an equal and respected member of such a community, will there by any fertile ground in which intransigent German nationalism could revive.

Such a community would not only be in itself a guarantee that Eastern fears of German revanchism had no validity. It would also have the economic and political strength to negotiate effectively with the Russians for better conditions in East Germany and the rest of Eastern Europe. And it would provide the Germans themselves with a political home: a framework within which they can look forward to a secure and honorable political future.

To the French, the political community would offer the only realistic hope of a more equal relationship with the United States. Any idea that, with Mr. Nixon in the White House, France will be able to develop a special relation with America would lead only to disappointment. No such special relation could be satisfactory, whether with Britain, France or any other European country alone, because the facts of size and of power are against it. The Americans will inevitably dominate any relationship with Europeans, unless we Europeans unite so as to give ourselves the necessary weight and strength.

This would not weaken or undermine the Atlantic Alliance. The French government itself has never gone so far as to denounce the Alliance. There is no reason to think that the Americans would be disturbed by a more united and active European partner in the Alliance. Europe would certainly have its differences with America. One of the main purposes of a united Europe would be to see that, when this happens, the European view cuts a lot more ice than it does today. The Alliance will never be satisfactory while it consists of fourteen states of which one—America—is so much larger and more powerful than the others. This has been shown for example by the American decisions on an antiballistic missile screen. Such a screen has profound implications for the security of Europe; yet decisions to build it, and subsequently to freeze work on it, have been taken without a scrap of prior consultation. Only if there is greater equality can we expect proper consultation and joint decisions. Only then will the relationship between the two sides of the Atlantic become stable and strong.

For the smaller countries of Europe, a political community, organized on a democratic basis, offers the only way to avoid dependence on one or other of the Continent's larger powers: France today, almost certainly Germany tomorrow. It has been suggested, in justification of the veto, that we would be a destabilizing element in the European community. But the opposite is the case. It is the composition of the EEC today that is unstable, because each smaller country is faced with the choice of supporting one or other of the "Big Two"—Germany or France. The danger of domination by the more powerful of the two provokes resentment on the part of the others. The current state of the EEC is not a good advertisement for this situation. Our presence would put an end to the possibility that any one country will dominate the Community; it would enable a new start to be made on a permanently democratic basis.

So the continental countries that would become members of the political community would all get substantial advantages from it. The prospect of more effective defense and a more powerful policy of détente would benefit Germany in particular, and justify the hope of a satisfactory solution to the German problem; greater equality with America would be of special interest to France; and a more democratic and stable political system, that could not be dominated by any one power, would attract the other countries on the Continent.

All these interests Britain shares. Britain has long worked for détente with the East, while not neglecting to safeguard our defense. We want more influence over America within the Atlantic Alliance, so that we can make sure the Alliance has a tenable defense program which has a meaning for Europe. A stable and democratic political system in Europe has always been one of our aims.

For us, in addition, it is of particular interest that a truly united Europe would have the capacity to give powerful support to the developing countries and to the construction of a stable world system within the United Nations. To take one example, 1 per cent of Britain's gross national product is about £400 million, while 1 per cent of the GNP of a European political community would be of the order of £2,000 million. The aid and assistance program of such a community could make a major impact on the economic growth of the developing countries in Asia, Africa and Latin America.

A Europe organized in this way could be more outward looking than either the EEC countries or Britain are able to be in the absence of real integration. As a part of a European political community, we would all share in the power to make a real contribution.

The community would be a regional organization as provided for under Article 52 of the United Nations Charter. The ultimate aim must be a United Nations that can enforce a world rule of law with the help of its own peace-keeping force. But the world is too deeply divided for this to be possible now. Meanwhile, therefore, we must press on with integration where it is possible—in Europe; and united Europe can play its part in supporting the United Nations and in working for the transformation of the UN into a real world authority.

An effective world role is beyond the reach of Britain or any other European country today. Nor can we act with any weight or authority in our relations with either super power. Tomorrow, unless we unite, we shall be overshadowed by China too. The EEC, since its development has been throttled, can do little to alter this. Unless we in Europe are to decline into insignificance, we must reverse this tide by organizing ourselves for common action: by establishing a European political community.

BLUEPRINT FOR UNITY IN EUROPE [7]

A blueprint has been made already for the united Europe it is hoped to build by enlarging the present Common Market.

Building starts next summer—provided details of the structure are acceptable to France and the cost is acceptable to Britain.

The design represents a halfway house between a free-trade area and a true union of states. It contains some surprises.

"It is a new deal for Western Europe—with three jokers in the pack," one European official explained to this correspondent.

The first of these "jokers" is the assurance given by West German Chancellor Willy Brandt to the Soviets, indirectly in public and directly in private, that whatever is built will not amount to "a new bloc." . . .

This appears to mean that, as with Lewis Carroll's Humpty-Dumpty, when European statesmen talk of "political union" they do so on the understanding that the words mean what they mean them to mean and nothing more.

The two other "jokers" are acceptance of the general rule of decisions by majority vote in the enlarged market's coun-

[7] From article by John Allan May, staff correspondent. *Christian Science Monitor.* p 1. D. 16, '69. Reprinted by permission from *The Christian Science Monitor* © 1969 The Christian Science Publishing Society. All rights reserved.

cil of ministers and a commitment to an elected European parliament.

The general rule of majority voting will be literally limited to the general. Each of the ten members—Belgium, France, Italy, Luxembourg, West Germany and the Netherlands plus Britain, Denmark, the Republic of Ireland, and Norway—will have a veto on particular matters of vital national concern, it is proposed.

The "European parliament" elected by universal suffrage will have strictly limited powers. These will mainly concern the budget of the Commission of the European Communities. There will be no power otherwise to legislate, no "governing party," no "opposition," no community executive.

This will not be a parliament in the normally accepted sense of the word. Nor, at first, will the unity of Europe be formalized in a union in the accepted constitutional sense.

In this context perhaps it should be stressed that the assurance that there is to be no "new bloc" is a requirement not only for the goodwill of the Soviet Union but even for the adhesion of both Britain and France to the "new Europe."

Prime Minister Harold Wilson and President Pompidou think alike on this. Both, indeed, think of it like former President Charles de Gaulle. It is to be a Europe of "nation states."

However, with these jokers uncovered, the rest of the pack makes a strong kind of sense.

Its other main points are:

The four applicants accept the Treaty of Rome and all the decisions taken under it since 1958.

They all enter together.

The enlarged market will be surrounded by a single tariff wall and will adopt a single commercial policy to countries and economic units outside that wall.

There will be completely free trade within the community thus formed. Free movement of peoples. Free movement for firms. Free movement of capital.

The common agricultural policy (CAP) will be redesigned.

The basic principles will remain the same: an organized farm market with common prices and a single system of trade; priority for commodities produced in the community; provision of community funds to modernize agriculture.

But the details will be renegotiated to reduce prices, surpluses, and costs, and to reconcile a formerly self-contained market having large exports with one now containing with it the world's greatest food importer—Britain.

New financial arrangements will be made to redistribute the burdens of the CAP fairly. And special arrangements will be made for West Indian sugar and New Zealand dairy products.

Two transitional periods are foreseen, one for full adhesion of the applicants to the CAP and another for their adhesion to the customs union. But it is hoped there will not be too great a time difference between the two periods.

Candidate countries [are] to agree to start at once pursuing policies convergent with those implemented within the community.

Candidates also join the European Coal and Steel Community, the European Atomic Community (Euratom), and the European Economic and Social Committee, and share common agreements with developing countries.

Candidates provide judges for the European court of justice and where necessary adapt their legal processes to the common European process in all matters covered by the Rome Treaty.

All members and applicants will take steps toward the completion of a monetary union.

This should lead to the holding of currency reserves in common, the harmonization of monetary policies and the regulation of currency parities on a community basis.

II. SHAPE OF PROSPERITY

EDITOR'S INTRODUCTION

Though the movement toward European economic unity has slowed down, Western Europe has continued to enjoy a rapid degree of expansion. The benefits of economic co-operation have been acknowledged by most Europeans, including former French President Charles de Gaulle. This section offers a view of Europe's economic prosperity and notes some of the important issues and problems connected with this growth.

The first article discusses a new economic boom which is sweeping across Europe. In West Germany alone there are nearly three quarters of a million unfilled jobs. Productive facilities are being expanded rapidly in order to keep up with rising demand. Italy, too, is in the midst of a fast-paced expansion. France and Britain, though beset by various political and social questions, are also moving toward new highs in standards of living and productivity.

The second article offers additional details on Europe's boom. This article explains how various countries are trying to control inflationary pressures, the by-product of rapid economic growth, by imposing selective price controls or regulating the amount of available money. In some respects, the economy of Western Europe is so vigorous it cannot escape being heated up to a dangerous degree.

The next article examines the numerous business mergers and cooperative arrangements which are taking place at an increasing rate in Western Europe so as to enable manufacturers to accumulate resources and facilities large enough to accommodate multicountry markets. The spark for this merger was the removal of the last remaining internal tariffs among the Common Market countries in 1968.

The following piece surveys the current economic scene in four countries: France, Italy, West Germany, and Britain. The last two articles offer brief comments on two areas in which the Common Market countries have made integration work. The first is in the construction of a continental highway system and the second is in the development of nuclear technology for peaceful purposes.

FUTURE OF EUROPE'S BOOM: MEANING TO U.S.[1]

A new economic boom is gathering momentum all across Europe.

Business optimism is on the rise—despite the political and financial uncertainty in France and elsewhere in the wake of President de Gaulle's departure.

The feeling among bankers and businessmen seems to be that come what may, Europe is heading into an upswing that will stretch well into 1970.

The Common Market nations of France, Germany, Italy, Belgium, the Netherlands and Luxembourg forecast an average growth rate this year [1969] of 6 per cent, highest since 1960. Other nations on the Continent expect to do at least as well. Even Britain looks for economic growth this year regardless of "Socialist austerity."

For the United States, all this is good news. Europe's expansion will mean stepped-up demand for American products. And European industry, with plenty of orders at home, may have less steel, other products to export, offer less competition in the U.S. market. The result could be a needed lift for the hard-hit U.S. trade balance.

Experts predict that Europe will buy nearly 12 billion dollars' worth of goods from the United States in 1969—about $1 billion more than last year.

[1] Reprinted from article in *U.S. News & World Report.* 66:30-1. My. 12, '69.

Sunshine and Clouds

The European picture today is full of paradoxes.

The forecasts of strong gains come amidst exceptional political instability and new pressures in the money markets.

France, though it has avoided the chaos that had been predicted by General de Gaulle, faces an unsure future. Italy is swept by violence and threatened by yet another government crisis. . . . Britain, numbed by four years of economic extremities, faces labor unrest and possible political turmoil.

Yet, there is widespread belief that the economy in these countries will achieve healthy growth in the year ahead. . . .

In 1968 France was rocked by a student revolt and workers' general strike, followed by financial crisis. Italy endured a government upheaval and student violence. West Germany was shaken by the Soviet invasion of neighboring Czechoslovakia. Two monetary scares precipitated massive runs out of the British pound sterling.

Still, Western Europe achieved a striking rate of economic expansion last year—and this year, say the experts, will be even better.

Why all the confidence? Says a Zurich banker:

Businessmen in Europe as in America no longer seem to fear a serious economic slump.

The prevailing view today is that governments and central banks simply cannot tolerate a bad recession and mass unemployment.

Unstable conditions for the French franc and the British pound cause some concern about the outlook, but it's felt that a new wave of currency speculation would not alter the generally bright picture for Europe's economy.

As an economist in Geneva put it:

A moderate devaluation of the French franc or a revaluation of the German mark would not reverse the upward movement in Europe's economy, at least not this year. [This analysis has proven correct.—Ed.]

The strong trend of business growth in Europe shows up in key countries.

German Power

Spending by consumers and by business in West Germany will stoke the most powerful economy on the Continent.

German industry already is operating close to capacity. Labor shortages are a problem. At latest count there were 720,000 unfilled jobs—three times the number of unemployed.

Wages and salaries keep rising at a rapid clip, with the gain this year seen reaching 9 to 10 per cent. As paychecks get fatter, consumers are going on a spending spree.

To keep up, business is expanding its facilities. New orders for capital goods are up 28 per cent so far this year. Steel orders alone have risen 25 per cent.

As the boom gets rolling, rising costs and heavy demand are putting upward pressure on prices. Living costs in Germany this year will escalate by about 3 per cent.

To combat forces for inflation, Germany's central bank now is moving to tighten supplies of money and credit. The squeeze, however, is not foreseen as severe enough to halt the strong upswing in business.

The German export boom is slowing a little. Heavy demand at home and longer waits for delivery inside Germany are tending to pull in imports. This year, say German trade experts, imports of foreign goods may rise 15 per cent.

French Comeback

A strong business recovery has been under way in France since last summer [1968] and the outlook remains good. Total output of goods and services is running about 8 per cent higher than a year ago. Profits are better than expected after the "wage explosion" of last year.

Order books of industry are filled. Unemployment has been dropping slowly. Skilled workers are in short supply.

The feeling that inflation is perpetual . . . tends to stimulate businessmen to buy and build now. Consumers in

France are spending freely for everything from cars to clothing.

The French government has clamped down on spending and on credit to prevent a runaway boom. Interest rates are up all along the line.

Sums up a Swiss observer:

"On the whole, the French situation is encouraging. It is much better today than people expected six months ago."

Italian Upswing

The upswing got under way last autumn and is still moving fast. The main worries for Italy are not economic. They are social unrest and political instability.

To head off some of the unrest, Italy has just introduced a new social security program. Pensions are being increased by $825 million this year.

The government and private industry are believed willing to accept union demands for hefty increases in pay.

Wages are seen rising by at least 10 per cent in the next 12 months. Consumer spending, as a consequence, can be expected to give strong support to the Italian economy in months ahead.

Businessmen are optimistic about the outlook despite a rash of illegal strikes, factory occupations and violence. Their order books are amply filled.

Italy's big surplus in trade is tending to shrink. Exports were up 20 per cent in the first two months of the year, but imports soared 31 per cent.

A related problem: heavy outflow of capital from Italy. Investors are shipping money out to take advantage of attractive interest rates available in the Euro-bond market. Added funds have been leaving the country in large amounts in fear that social turmoil could lead to riots and near-revolution as in France in 1968.

The Bank of Italy is striving to stem the flow of capital out of the country.

Commented one observer in nearby Switzerland:

Italy's industry is going ahead at top speed. But the social and political climate is worsening. I don't see serious trouble for the lira yet, but the period of economic stability may be coming to an end.

Britain's Troubles

Great Britain is the most serious soft spot among major European nations. The Labour government is desperately trying to hold down domestic consumption and stimulate exports in an effort to achieve the first balance-of-payments surplus since 1963. The prospect of success this year [1969] is by no means certain.

The government is budgeting for an increase of slightly less than 3 per cent in total output. Hope is that growth will come almost entirely from rising exports and private investment, not from expanded consumer demand at home.

If domestic demand increases faster than planned—which many private economists expect—the economy may become overheated in the autumn. Such an outcome would confront the government with the need to impose still more tax increases and possibly import controls.

The outlook for Britain is for modest economic gains, relatively full employment, a slow rise in living standards.

Prospects: Rosy

Thus, all in all, Western Europe is looking ahead confidently to healthy growth in business well into next year.

EUROPE TRIES TO KEEP ITS BOOM IN BALANCE [2]

Lobsters were available in only the most exclusive food shops in West Germany a year ago. Today, in German supermarkets, they are selling like bratwurst, at $4 frozen, $25 live.

[2] Article in *Business Week*. p 128-30. My. 10, '69. Reprinted from May 10, 1969 issue of *Business Week* by special permission. Copyrighted © 1969 by McGraw-Hill, Inc.

Hausfraus tucking such delicacies into chock-full grocery carts have their counterparts all over Europe—from the Dutch charwoman who just packed husband and children into a new car and camping trailer for a vacation in sunny Spain, to the French policemen joining a six-month waiting list to buy Ford's jaunty Capri coupe.

Happy Days

With new signs of prosperity popping out faster than the blossoms of a late spring, Europe is in the midst of a business upturn so vigorous that only the wariest observers refuse to call it a boom. Not since the early years of the Common Market, when trade barriers were falling fast and companies were eagerly grabbing for new markets, has business been so good in so many countries.

West Germany, its "economic miracle" restored after a crushing recession, still is riding a wave of prosperity that scored a growth rate of 7 per cent in real terms last year [1968].

In France, consumers have all but ignored government attempts to dampen spending in the aftermath of the franc crisis last fall. Estimates of real economic growth for this year have just been revised upward to 5.8 per cent.

Italy's consumers are stepping out, too, and the economy is responding: Industrial production in January and February was 6.4 per cent ahead of last year.

Reacting to the ebullience of Europe's biggest industrial powers, other countries—including Belgium, Holland, Switzerland, and Sweden—are racing ahead as well. And businessmen in every corner of Europe are making the most of some golden opportunities.

Roaring Ahead

"Business is great—in capital letters," says a Ford of Germany spokesman who reflects the euphoria that permeates some of Europe's biggest companies. In the first quarter of 1969, Ford sold 56 per cent more cars in the Common Market than in the same period last year.

Other companies are just as happy. Worldwide sales of Hoechst, the German chemical giant, were up 21 per cent in the first quarter of this year compared with 1968. Domestic sales rose 17 per cent. "We're already operating at full capacity," says Hoechst chief executive Karl Winnacker. "But we are determined to expand our capacity as rapidly as we can."

The upsurge has soaked up so much steel capacity that European mills, which just last year agreed to limit their exports to the United States, have started buying some semifinished products from American producers.

The new outburst of prosperity may never expand to the size of earlier European booms. Political uncertainties in France and the growing conviction that exchange rates will be revised are clouding the business outlook. Devaluation of the franc would raise import prices for France, and might accelerate French inflation. Revaluation of the mark could slow the pace of Germany's expansion a bit—while helping other Common Market exporters. [The French franc and the German mark were subsequently revalued.—Ed.]

The Brakes

But boom-and-bust cycles earlier this decade taught Europe some hard lessons about controlling growth and avoiding recessions. And it's beginning to look as though these lessons are being applied.

Three years ago the German Bundesbank waited until a downturn had started before raising interest rates. Many economists say this cascaded the slow-down into the full-scale 1966-67 recession. This time the Bundesbank is not waiting: As consumer spending zoomed, it has just sought to slow it by raising the discount rate to 4 per cent.

In another hedge against inflation, Bonn has squeezed federal controls on the budgets of West Germany's twelve federated states, to curb their expenditures for public projects.

Meanwhile, in France, the austerity program initiated by the Gaullist government six months ago [December 1968] may be beginning to have some effect. Even so, administrators are putting together a package of measures now, to tighten installment buying terms for consumers and restrict the short-term money market for corporate borrowers.

The Dutch have clamped on price controls for the first time since the war because of a price rise fueled by consumer spending, and they raised the bank rate to 5.5 per cent. Italy, on the other hand, is keeping interest rates low and is continuing the judicious pump priming that has pulled the country from recession to near boom in the past three years.

How It Began

In most of Europe, prosperity's big push started last year with sharp jumps in consumer spending, capital investment, and exports. Clear evidence that a boom was in the making came in the last quarter when the Common Market's rate of growth in industrial production hit 12 per cent on an annual basis—highest in its history.

In France, management launched a production offensive to recoup losses caused by the May-June riots. In Germany, production rose with the general buoyancy that followed the 1966-67 recession. In Holland and Belgium production was stimulated by the infectious influence of Germany's recovery.

Exports took much of the Common Market's additional industrial output. With the ending of internal tariffs last July [1968], trade within the community increased 14 per cent. Exports outside the Continent climbed 12 per cent as American inflation helped increase the Common Market's exports to the United States and widened the price advantage of European goods over U.S. merchandise in third countries.

Chronologically, the first consumers to go on a spending binge were the French. Big raises won by France's workers pushed consumer demand, and fears of devaluation added to the frenzy of buying. In December, government economic managers launched a series of austerity measures to slow things down, and the consumer boom in France may now have passed its peak.

France Strains

French consumer-goods producers are probably a bit relieved. Radio and TV set manufacturers, for example, depleted their stocks by the end of 1968. Since then, a shortage of electronic components has prevented them from building up their inventories of sets. . . .

Before buying trailed off in home appliances, sales had risen some 15 per cent during the first quarter of this year. French auto production was up 5 per cent in the first quarter, but Renault notes that almost all of its 10 per cent production increase was absorbed by the export market.

French business is brightest in the basic industries. Chemicals are setting the pace with sales in the first quarter 19 per cent ahead of 1968. Steel production is running at 90 per cent of capacity and sales in the first quarter were up 5 per cent.

Germany Zooms

In Germany, the boom is in full swing. Industrial production is running at 88 per cent of capacity, highest since 1961, and the affluent German consumer is having a field day. Grundig in Nuremburg is turning out color TV sets at full capacity; its wholesalers are moving them faster than Grundig can fill orders, and now the company is running into a transistor shortage.

Most of Grundig's color TV customers are buying its most expensive set—a model costing $550. "It surprised us," says Herman Reichel, a business analyst at Grundig. "We had expected our medium-priced set to sell best."

Says a BMW car dealer in Bonn: "Just six months ago, people were buying our smaller models and financing about 60 per cent of the price. Now they choose the larger models, like our 2000 Tilux (price: $3,125), and plop down the full price in cash."

At the Hamburg boat show last January, sales outstripped the most optimistic predictions of the exhibitors—more than double the sales at the 1968 show.

Behind the glittering consumer boom in Germany, capital investment outlays also are soaring. In the machine tool industry, the order backlog stood at seven months in February. Manufacturers expect it to move close to nine months before the year is out, the highest level in eight years.

Holland, Belgium

Of the six Common Market countries, Holland is closest to having a genuinely overheated economy. Its price freeze last month [April 1969], rolling back prices to the level of March 14, was a tough response to spiraling inflation. (One reason for the swift escalation of prices in Holland and Germany is that both countries recently switched to the French-style value-added tax. Many retailers grabbed this chance to raise their prices by more than the amount of the tax increase.) Despite the price freeze, Holland expects a 7 per cent rise in the cost of living this year—enough to wipe out wage hikes Dutch workers got earlier in the year.

Germany and Holland also have in common the biggest labor shortages in the Common Market. As delivery times lengthen, both countries are drawing more heavily on workers from Italy, Spain, Turkey, Greece, Yugoslavia, and Morocco.

Belgium so far has escaped the vicious inflation Holland has experienced, but it will go to the value-added tax next January, and some price increases are expected before then as consumers try to beat the tax. In addition, Belgian companies are approaching capacity production and planning to step up investment spending by 17 per cent over last year. "Business is good," says a Belgian chemical industry spokesman, "but I wouldn't call it a boom." Nonetheless, he expects a rise in profits of more than 5 per cent this year.

Italy Relaxed

In Italy, Fiat's new 128 sedan is expected to touch off a flurry of new-car purchases, as any new Fiat model nearly always does. Auto production is already up nearly 14 per cent over last year.

But Italy's new prosperity so far is more sober than the frenzied spending that marked the 1962-63 boom. In those days, consumers spent a lot on ostentation—cars, apartments, yachts. This time, they are spending more carefully.

Prices are still relatively stable in Italy. A new round of wage demands is expected before the end of the year, however, and prices could well start turning up in 1970.

Repercussions

The business bustle in Europe is being felt by the Common Market's trading partners. British exports to the Six were up 28.5 per cent last year, with Germany, Belgium, and Holland the biggest buyers. The German boom helped push Switzerland's foreign trade to a 12 per cent gain last year, and Sweden boosted its exports to the Common Market by 14 per cent.

Among other signs of the upturn: European visitors to the United States last year topped 1 million for the first time, nearly 250,000 more than in 1967, making it the biggest annual increase in history. More continental Europeans also visited Britain last year, helping the British earn their first payments surplus from tourism.

EUROPE'S MERGER BOOM THUNDERS
A LOT LOUDER [3]

"A kind of gigantomania seems to have set in."

That's the comment of a West German economist on the wave of mergers and cooperative arrangements that is tossing up powerful new industrial concentrations in Europe. In nations from Sweden to Italy, more and more companies are

[3] Article in *Business Week*. p 53-6. N. 23, '68. Reprinted from the November 23, 1968 issue of *Business Week* by special permission. Copyrighted © 1968 by McGraw-Hill, Inc.

merging, swapping stock, forming joint ventures, and working together in manufacturing, sales, and research and development.

A massive push to the trend is the need to achieve the size to enable European companies to compete with U.S. giants in ever-growing markets, to cut production costs, and to pool their financial and technological resources to develop costly new high-technology products.

The pressure rose . . . as the last remaining internal tariffs were removed in the Common Market. This cuts the chances of survival for companies that have lived off limited markets, behind the shields of national tariffs. And it stirred individual governments to push the trend to concentration, lest key industries wither away because they are too small to compete.

Stay-at-Home

So far, the mergers have been pretty well confined within national borders, but now the get-together spirit is beginning to take on some intra-European aspects, despite the jealous guardianship of national authorities. With real mergers all but impossible, the cross-border moves have generally taken the form of agreements and cooperation; such deals are cropping up in such crucial industries as aircraft, autos, steel, and chemicals.

For U.S. companies operating in Europe, all this means dealing with tougher competitors who no longer think exclusively of national markets. And as mergers gobble up hundreds of small companies, there are fewer left for Americans to make deals with. . . .

Both inside and outside the Common Market, mergers are coming fast. Final arrangements [which were completed in 1969] are being made for one of Britain's biggest mergers: the fusing . . . of General Electric Co. of Britain (no relation to GE in the United States) and English Electric Co. Together, they will have sales of about $2 billion.

On the Continent, . . . two of France's big chemical companies, Ugine Kuhlmann and Saint Gobain, announced that they will merge affiliates to constitute one of Europe's biggest fertilizer companies. Two sizable Belgian steel companies, Cockerill-Ougree-Providence and Esperance-Longdoz, decided to pool investments to pep up profits; they probably will merge eventually. Earlier this month, BASF, one of Germany's biggest chemical companies, took over Wintershall, a $375 million oil refiner and potassium producer.

Still more linkups are on the horizon. Electronics maker Société Alsthom is expected to be taken over by one of the two big French electrical-electronics companies. The West German government is pushing some small domestic oil companies together to form the first big all-German company in the industry. In Italy, two big petrochemicals makers, Società Italiana Resine and Rumianca, probably will merge.

The Big One

Europe's most eye-popping industrial move of the year so far—and an omen for the future—was the Italian Fiat's bid for a stake in Citroën, an ailing French auto maker, Fiat's chairman, Giovanni Agnelli, believes European auto makers must merge across borders if they are to compete with Detroit's Big Three. This time, the Fiat effort was beaten back by France's President de Gaulle; Fiat had to settle for a 15 per cent interest in Citroën, plus the forming of a jointly owned company to cooperate in certain technical and commercial areas.

Despite Fiat's failure, the deal shook up other European auto makers; they still think Fiat will eventually get control. In reaction, Renault and Peugeot, already cooperating in purchasing raw materials and in research, began groping for ways to achieve more significant economies.

Computers

Automobiles aren't the only sector in which formation of companies that straddle Europe's national borders is considered inevitable. Jacques Maillet, president of Cie. Inter-

nationale pour L'Informatique—the all-French computer
company—believes European computer manufacturers inevitably will band together to compete with U. S. giants, at
least in supersized machines. As for steel, national concentrations have gone so far that across-border agreements, particularly in big new investments, probably will come fairly
soon. Holland's Hoogovens already owns 15 per cent of
Hoesch, a major West German producer.

Nationalism

Plenty of companies in Europe clearly want to get together, but for a while they will be facing assorted obstacles.
It's hard to form a truly "European" company inside the
Common Market because the EEC has no company law. A
model company statute has been drawn up and discussed,
but the Six haven't composed many of their differences:
Some big fiscal and other hurdles must be cleared.

The main "European" get-together in recent times has
been between Germany's Agfa and Belgium's Gevaert in the
photo products field. They created two separate jointly-
owned companies, which has brought some benefits, but
which falls short of true merger. No other major companies
have as yet followed suit.

Bogey of Nationalism

The most important obstacle, of course, is economic nationalism—as many U.S. companies have already discovered
in Europe. When Fiat tried to take over Citroën, for example, the French people as well as their government resented the idea. Says . . . [the] editor of the business monthly,
L'Expansion: "For many Frenchmen, Citroën is somewhat
like Alsace-Lorraine. You don't easily surrender such a prestigious industry."

Facing that sort of resistance, European companies that
seek to reach across borders tend to settle on their own initiative for cooperative arrangements that fall short of merger.
In aerospace, there is already substantial cross-frontier co-

operation: France's Dassault recently announced plans with Italy's Fiat and Germany's Dornier to work together on two new airframe projects.

Among the other industries in which cooperation deals are being made:

In chemicals, Hoeschst bought a minority interest in French drug maker Roussel-Uclaf, and the two companies agreed to cooperate worldwide in research, production, and marketing. Roussel also has linked its sales and production operations with Boehringer Mannheim, Germany's third largest maker of pharmaceuticals.

In metallurgy, Rothschild-controlled Pennaroya, a $200 million French producer of copper, zinc, lead, nickel, and other metals, is setting up a 50-50 joint company with West Germany's Preussag, a powerful holding company.

In machinery, Demag, one of Germany's biggest producers, and Richier, which has 35 per cent of the French market for construction machinery, will cooperate in marketing, joint planning, R&D [research and development], and the exchange of knowhow.

Such limited working arrangements seem to suit many European industrialists. Says Roussel-Uclaf President . . . : "Frankly, we like the idea of European partnership of this sort—we have not only real cooperation with a big competitor, but we remain independent."

The Execution

Obviously, the effectiveness of these agreements depends on the way the companies carry them out. "They are like treaties, which can be extremely impressive on paper, but ultimately it is in the concrete act of getting together that the significant action takes place," notes a top executive of Rhone-Poulenc, France's chemical-textile-pharmaceuticals giant and the biggest competitor of Roussel-Uclaf.

Meantime, mergers have been occurring inside European national boundaries at a hectic pace.

72   The Reference Shelf

In France alone over the past six years, it's estimated that small and medium-size companies have been merging at the rate of 1,800 to 2,000 annually. In West Germany, where only large corporations bent on merger are required to notify the Bonn government, the number of such notifications reached 65 in 1967, up from 29 in 1963. In Sweden, mergers and other industrial linkups rose from 64 in 1958 to 341 in 1966, then fell off to 259 last year. In Italy, from 1961 to 1967, there were 176 major mergers.

The Focus on Britain

Certainly, the focus of merger activity in Europe in recent times has been Britain. Pushed by the need to be more competitive, whole British industries—shipbuilding, steel aircraft, machine tools, and computers among them—have restructured, or are being regrouped through mergers and takeovers. This year may bring the flood tide of giant mergers. Money spent by British companies on mergers and acquisitions in 1968 is expected to hit a record $3.5 billion.

One businessman figures that one out of every five British manufacturing companies will be absorbed by other companies in the next decade. British industry still is highly fragmented; the nation has two thirds as many manufacturing enterprises as the United States with only a third as much population.

Many of the mergers have been pushed along by a government agency, the Industrial Reorganization Corporation. At the moment, IRC is involved in reorganizing the nuclear industry, compressing four reactor builders into two new companies. IRC also plans to look closely at such metalworking industries as mining machinery, pumps, pressure vessels, textile machines, and plastics machinery.

Appliances

In France, too, the government has been pushing industry to consolidate for greater strength. Most notably, the scattered electronics and appliance industry, has recently become dominated by one merger-minded monolith: Cie. Française Thomson-Houston Hotchkiss-Brandt, better known simply as Thomson-Brandt.

Pushed by the government, Thomson-Brandt this year acquired its major competitors, Claret in appliances and CSF in electronic equipment. Both Claret and CSF had been losing money heavily; Claret, like Thomson-Brandt itself, has been badly hurt by Italian competitors, who sold 473,000 refrigerators in France last year. Now, with lower prices possible and a service network superior to those of the Italian companies, Thomson-Brandt thinks it can stem the Italian inundation.

In steel, too, the Paris government has been promoting mergers to create two big combines in France. This year, three steel companies in eastern France got together—De Wendel, Sidelor, and Mosellane. Combined, their sales total $744 million. Now specialty steel producers are starting a similar regrouping.

In Germany, the Bonn government has made "konzentration" its favorite game. Shipbuilding is already concentrated; now the government is working on the aircraft industry, where Messerschmidt and Boelkow have merged.

In other sectors, some of the biggest German companies are getting together, Siemens and AEG-Telefunken—the nation's No. 1 and No. 2 electrical companies—plan to pool their power generating business; it could lead to merger. In steel, cooperative deals are aimed at cutting costs. Thus Mannesman is renting rolling mill capacity from Thyssen, which will have capacity to spare until 1973. By then, Mannesman and Hoesch will be using a new mill they are building jointly.

Auto Trio

As for autos, the three all-German-owned companies—Volkswagen, Daimler-Benz, and BMW—can probably hold out separately for a while. But VW officials expect that in five to ten years the industry will be narrowed down to one big company, centered around VW and Daimler-Benz.

BMW, small but profitable, has already made known that it is interested in talking to would-be partners. "We would make a very rich bride," says Paul G. Hahnemann, a director.

Germany already has three of Europe's most powerful chemical companies—Hoechst, Bayer, and BASF—which are all gobbling up other companies. Bayer is trying to get control of Huels, the No. 4 producer, while Cassella, No. 5, may go to Hoechst. BASF has taken over Nordmark Werke.

In Italy, mergers are continuing to sweep the auto and chemical industries. The nation's private business was alarmed a few weeks ago when the state-owned ENI (oil) and IRI (holding company) acquired near control of Montecatini Edison, Italy's largest industrial company.

Sweden is giving high national precedence to merging small, marginal companies, especially in the vital pulp and paper industry, where the United States is beginning to invade Sweden's markets in Europe.

Voice of Dissent

Some of Europe's biggest industrialists still resist the merger tide. "Don't forget," says chairman Giuseppe Luraghi of Italy's Alfa Romeo, "that size isn't everything. If you have a personalized product—like the Alfa Romeo—you have to keep the personality of the product. Efficiency is what counts."

It may be noted that Luraghi has another reason for not fearing that another company will take him over: Alfa Romeo is controlled by the Italian government.

EUROPEAN ECONOMY [4]

France

Last year [1969] was a hectic and unsettling one and this year promises to be more of the same.

[4] From article "European Economy: A Special Report," by Henry Giniger, Robert C. Doty, Dan Morgan, Alfred Friendly, American foreign correspondents. *International Herald Tribune.* p 7. Ja. 16, '70. Reprinted by permission.

The resignation of President Charles de Gaulle last April and his replacement two months later by Georges Pompidou, his former premier, marked more than a political change. Suddenly the country became preoccupied with its economic well-being after eleven years of a man and a style that gave an appearance of world power and solid strength.

The appearance had been jarred a year before when discontent by students and workers produced riots, a paralysis in industrial production and public services, and a near collapse of the regime.

General de Gaulle had still been unable to devalue the franc despite the speculation against it and the enormous drain on France's once fat reserves. By the time Mr. Pompidou took office, the outflow of funds and the discount of the franc in money markets was such that he felt obliged in August to decree as his first emergency measure a 12.5 per cent devaluation.

A few weeks later the government drew up a belt-tightening program involving severe credit restrictions, a reduction in the rate of increase of public spending so as to produce a balanced budget, and measures to encourage private savings.

The goal was to reduce internal consumption and to transfer industrial production to the export market so that by the middle of 1970 inflation would be brought under control at home and balance established in trade abroad.

Officials began the new year in relative euphoria because the program was working better and faster than they had expected. A balanced budget was voted by parliament, private savings set a record, exports were covering 90 per cent and more of imports by the end of the year, the rate of internal spending showed a tendency to drop, and prices, if not completely stable, did not spur out of control.

The economy recorded an estimated increase of 8.3 per cent in the gross national product. There was virtually full employment with industry complaining of a shortage of trained personnel.

But beyond the short-range concern for the country's finances lay serious long-range concerns about structural weaknesses. Wide discontent underlined the gravity of these weaknesses.

The country was told, for example, that in the year of wide-open competition France had entered, it did not have adequate industrial structures. Premier Jacques Chaban-Delmas said that France could not play a world role until it had developed a fully competitive industry. A noticeable trend toward industrial mergers indicated that industrialists were taking the problem seriously.

It was believed that the trend toward concentration, involving the merger of some companies and the disappearance of others, would continue. Many economists saw the salvation of French industry, in part at least, in the Common Market.

Agriculture was also in a difficult transitional period. Most experts recognized that France still had too many peasants and that the need to concentrate and modernize was as great in agriculture as it was in industry.

Perhaps half the active rural population of about three million will have to move off the farms, and this will give the country a source of manpower for the years ahead provided its school facilities are able to train the newcomers.

The small shopkeeper and artisan were also threatened by the trend to concentration and efficiency. Chain stores and supermarkets are becoming increasingly part of the landscape, but what may be lost in intimacy and the personal touch may be gained in fairer prices for consumers.

In the meantime, unrest made the country aware that changes were afoot and that the transitional phase could be a painful one.

Italy

The healthy glow that has suffused the face of Italy for the last four years began to take on something of a hectic flush at the end of 1969, threatening a bout of inflation fever for 1970.

Strikes throughout the fall cut production and reduced the growth rate from an anticipated 6 to 7 per cent to about 5.4 per cent, still a respectable rate. But strike settlement terms will increase labor costs this year by an estimated 16 to 17 per cent.

If industry tries to pass on higher labor costs to consumers, it will both speed up the inflationary cycle and reduce its ability to compete in export markets.

These factors have moved Treasury Minister Emilio Colombo, who, with Governor Guido Carli of the Bank of Italy, has guided the nation through most of the 1963-64 slump and through the recent fat years, to remark that a "clearly difficult situation" faces the nation this year.

The increase in labor costs, he said, "cannot in any way be equaled by increased production."

The squeeze will be tightest on those sectors of the economy largely dependent on export markets. They are confronted with competitive world market prices at a time when labor costs have soared.

One noted economic analyst foresees the possibility that "Italy will have the sad distinction of experiencing both inflation and increased unemployment."

He reasons that inflation and wage rises result in a shortage of investment capital to expand production. At the same time, he says, a predicted decline in construction will produce large layoffs, and efforts by industrial management to counteract the wage rises by technological improvements will reduce their labor needs.

Chances for parrying these threats depend on two imponderables.

First, the nation's economic managers must achieve more success than they have had thus far in checking the flight of capital abroad. This movement—estimated to have drained $3.92 billion out of Italy last year—is motivated primarily by the search for higher interest rates abroad rather than by the political-economic panic that produced a similar phenomenon in 1963.

Suggested remedies . . . include new laws to ease the issuance of new stocks and make them attractive to investors and to authorize the formation and sale of mutual funds.

And Mr. Carli may seek to check or reverse the capital flow by counseling issuance of Italian bonds—there have already been several—on the Eurodollar market, letting prices of state bonds sag to increase their yield or applying a credit squeeze to make Italian interest rates competitive with those that have been attracting capital abroad.

The practicability and efficacy of some of these measures are linked to the second imponderable—the Italian political scene.

When the Socialists first entered the government in 1963, their entry fee was acquiescence in a Carli-Colombo deflationary program that produced unpopular wage controls and increased unemployment.

Today, on the brink of a new governing alliance with the Christian Democrats, the Socialists are unlikely to take the plunge unless they get assurances that they will not again be identified with an economic austerity program that would alienate the Socialist electorate.

Another political factor bearing on the chances of effective economic management is the flirtation of Socialists and left-wing Christian Democrats with the Communists for some form of "opening," "dialogue," or "understanding." Any notable advance by the Communists towards even a peripheral voice in governmental decisions would speedily undermine confidence in the business-financial community.

West Germany

Currency revaluation, West Germany's big domestic political issue in 1969, is destined to be the big economic issue of 1970.

All the experts agree that the October revaluation—which was held up for months by the Christian Democrats until they were dumped from power in a national election—

will cool off an overheated situation, and prevent a really severe inflation.

But when, and how much? That is the question that not even Social Democratic Economics Minister Karl Schiller can answer with any certainty.

The revaluation—of 8.5 per cent, or 9.3 per cent on a mark to dollars conversion—is the key element in Mr. Schiller's program of "stabilization without stagnation." It is now conceded by politicians here that the signs pointing toward such a step were so strong in October that had the election gone differently even the CDU would have taken it, although probably the rate would have been smaller.

Industrial prices in the months before October were rising at a rate of 6 per cent a year—a level not reached since the boom period of the Korean War. Industry was chugging away at 90 per cent or more of capacity and the number of foreign workers had hit the 1.5 million level, after dropping below 1 million in 1967.

The strong expansion, moreover, had led to a clamor for wage increases that had not been heard since the end of the war. The waves of wildcat strikes which hit before the election were a clear sign that the postwar era of industrial peace was over and that the fat, establishment-linked West German trade unions, whose membership has not increased in a decade, were in plenty of trouble on the shop floors.

All this was plenty worrisome to Germans who more than almost any Europeans are allergic to inflation and economic disorder.

The currency change was aimed at the core of the problem—the country's huge overseas trade surplus—which came to more than $4 billion in 1969. . . .

Theoretically, the effect of revaluation should be to encourage foreign imports, thus increasing local competition and driving down prices, and to slow the export boom. But German industry has a tradition of hanging on to its export markets at all costs, and there have been few signs yet of a slowdown.

Forecasters of the Organization for Economic Cooperation and Development in Paris say there is no reason to expect any weakening of demand pressures in the country until at least mid-1970. Year-end tax cuts leave plenty of money around for spending.

The Paris analysts predict a growth in volume of 6 per cent in the first half of 1970, declining to 4 per cent in the second. But the general expectation is that wage increases will far outstrip productivity for the second year in a row, which could maintain the upward pressure on prices. Germans, for once, are in a spending mood.

By most standards the 2 to 3 per cent inflation in 1969 was not severe, and it was felt mostly in the area of foods. Nevertheless, Mr. Schiller had called for concerted action on the price front, including holding down public spending, encouraging savings and drafting the Federal Cartel Office into service to take all administrative steps it can to increase domestic competition.

He can already claim success in the monetary field. For the revaluation has succeeded in draining out of the country most, if not all, of the $5 billion in foreign funds which poured in to buy marks between February and September, in expectation of a revaluation. This, coupled with restrictive central bank measures, has resulted in a decrease in bank liquidity.

But forecasters doubt that tight money policies would be pursued to a point where they would affect employment significantly.

Britain

A toothache may not be the most important thing in the world, Roy Jenkins, British Chancellor of the Exchequer, observes. But while you have it, you can't think of very much else.

Britain has had a toothache, in the form of a deficit in its balance of international payments, every year since 1962. It has not had a respectable surplus since 1958. And it hasn't been able to think of anything else.

Now it has a surplus, running during the third quarter of 1969 at an annual rate of about $1.2 billion and, even after a deficit first quarter, making virtually certain Mr. Jenkins's promise to Britain of a $750 million surplus for the financial year as a whole (ending March, 31, [1970]).

Dare the nation hope that at long last, and for some time to come, it has broken the agonizing "stop-go" jerks of a plagued economy?

The surplus was achieved by a ferocious credit squeeze, a sharply deflationary fiscal policy with steeply increased income and other taxes, and downward pressure on investment. Now the question is: Can that international payments surplus be maintained—to pay off the huge stack of foreign debts that have piled up against Britain?

The answer is not entirely in Britain's hands.

That part of it out of U.K. control has to do with the course of world trade in 1970—especially U.S. trade. If there is a recession in the United States or sharp deflation with a serious deceleration of growth—even to the zero level, as looks possible from here—the consequences to the rising line on Britain's export chart would be very dangerous indeed.

The part of the answer that does remain in Britain's hands—in theory, if not in political reality—has to do with wage and price control here.

The pressure for wage increases is now uncontainable, wages will rise in 1970, and the only uncertainty is by how much, and how soon prices will catch up with them. Britain thus has the miserable potential of once again pricing herself out of the export market and—by reason of increased home demand from bigger pay checks—consuming itself out of it.

If that potential comes to reality, Britain will be back again where it was, losing reserves and having to impose the chill cure for its fever.

The government has set the permissible norms for the next round of wage increases from 2.5 to 4.5 per cent. But that is largely facade. Whether the Labour Party survives the

3

82   The Reference Shelf

election expected in the next twelve months, or whether the
Tories come to power, neither can hold pay increases to that
range.

The next round of wage contracts coming up—curiously
enough, mostly in the public sector rather than in private
manufacturing—are likely to result in boosts of 6 to 10 per
cent.

And if wage rises come, can price increases be far behind?

Luckily for Britain, its trading competitors are also suffering inflation. Wage costs have risen as much in France
and Japan, export prices in the United States even more.
Britain's costs and prices of export goods have grown "much
less"—the phrase is the Treasury's—than those of its competitors, and thanks to revaluation of the West German mark
and devaluation of the French franc, Britain's position will
be improved still further.

EEC MAKES HEADWAY ON HIGHWAYS [5]

While the European Common Market plan has been
nearly halted by repeated injections of political and economic rivalries, one sector—highways—continues to defy all
opponents.

Despite bitter disputes over agriculture, transport, and
standardized taxation, all six members of the EEC seem to
agree that the speedy expansion of the continental network
of roads is essential and that its long-term aim can go far
toward ultimate political and economic integration.

The steady progress of the Customs Union between the
countries is also serving as an impetus for accelerating construction of the many new long-distance highways which
have already been agreed upon by the respective countries.

The present program comprises ten major highways au-
thorized by the European Commission and seven being paid
for by the European Investment Bank.

[5] From article "EEC Makes Headway on New Highway Grid," by H. G.
Franks, journalist. *Christian Science Monitor.* p 14. Mr. 29, '69. Reprinted by
permission from *The Christian Science Monitor.* © 1969 The Christian Science
Publishing Society. All rights reserved.

In addition the Netherlands, Italy, France, and West Germany are implementing their own comprehensive road networks by making large amounts available for the next four or five years.

Commission Plan Mapped

The new highways sponsored by the European Commission . . . are:

1. A German motorway from Aachen to the Dutch border, thus considerably improving the outlet from the Netherlands (known as the gateway to Europe) into Germany, particularly the industrial Ruhr area, and Belgium

2. From Lübeck, Germany, to Puttgarden, providing the missing link in a highway running from the Pyrenees to the Baltic Sea and giving an excellent connection between the Common Market countries and Scandinavia

3. From Nuremberg to Regensburg in the eastern part of West Germany to improve connections for Dutch and Belgian traffic to Austria and Eastern Europe

4. From Montaubar in Germany to Luxembourg via Coblenz and Trier. . . [to] give much better connections between Germany, Luxembourg, and France and be a valuable linkup between the towns along the Moselle River

5. Ring road around Luxembourg City especially for international traffic

6. Reconstruction of German Highway 10, one of the main arteries of southern Germany . . . linking the Saarland with Augsburg, thus providing, an important connection between the Benelux countries, Austria, and Italy

Luxembourg Links

7. From Luxembourg to Saarbrücken to link up with the new Antwerp-Brussels-Luxembourg highway

8. From Arlon to Luxembourg and thence to the French border, adding another good link between France and Belgium

9. Luxembourg to Esch on the French border, to give better connections between mid-France and the more eastern and northern countries

10. From Strassen to Mersch in Luxembourg, mainly to open up a large new industrial area

The Investment Bank proposes the following:

A. The Brenner motorway across the Italian-Austrian border to link Milan, Rome, and Naples. The $24 million loan by the bank is intended to pay for the most difficult 55 miles of this route from Bolzano to the border.

B. The highway through the Aosta Valley as a final link in the road connecting Italy with France and Switzerland through the Mont Blanc and the Grand St. Bernard Tunnels, respectively. The bank's loan for this sector is $24 million.

Paris-Brussels Connection

C. Fast highway from Paris to Brussels. Though much of this on the French side is already finished, the bank is providing $16 million for a section between the French border and Houdeng in south Belgium.

D. Highway [from] Roquebrune to Menton as part of the main road between the French and Italian Rivieras. For this the bank is lending $10 million.

E. Highway from Savona to Ponte San Luigi in Italy to link up with project D and give good connection with Genoa.

F. Highway [from] Metz to Saarbrücken, for which $10 million is being provided.

G. Highway [from] Antwerp to the Dutch border, linking up with the main highway from Paris to Amsterdam.

While these combined operations are being carried out, most of the EEC countries are rapidly expanding their own national highways.

Italy is adding about 600 miles of fast highways to its network, at a cost of $1.4 billion. This will provide about 3,500 miles of four-lane or six-lane roads by 1972. In addition, a further $1.4 billion is earmarked for new roads to open up the Adriatic coast.

Bonn Pegs $11 billion

Germany's program provides for about 2,600 miles of fast highways by 1972, together with the construction of a further 3,000 miles between 1972 and 1985 at a cost of about $11 billion. When this network is finished every German town will be no more than thirty miles from a main highway. In the Ruhr area the maximum distance will be less than five miles.

France is not making quite such ambitious plans but is spending about $450 million a year in expanding or improving its present roads. The main feature of the French program is the construction of the fast Paris-Marseille highway, to be ready at the end of 1970. For the time being an important part of the road program is the improvement of communications in and around main cities, along with larger sums than usual being spent on maintenance.

Because of the ever-increasing goods and passenger traffic into and out of Holland as the gateway to Europe, the Netherlands government has just drawn up a new highway plan aimed at catering fully to the tremendous stream of traffic passing through its great ports of Rotterdam and Amsterdam, its international airport at Schiphol, and the spectacular addition of container transport to the daily freight services by roads fanning out from Dutch centers to all parts of Europe.

Dutch Speed Plans

This plan is to be finally implemented by 1978. All its major sections are being speeded up so that more than half will be completed by the time the main extension of the European highway development program is ready, by about 1972.

This means that, despite its geographical smallness, there will be 2,500 miles of good highways in the Netherlands. More than half will be specially designed for fast through traffic.

The total cost of this new network will be about $2.8 billion. It will include a large number of tunnels and bridges to cope with the already dense waterway network of the country.

The outstanding feature of the whole European road-extension program is the way in which the six Common Market countries have cooperated. This has covered not only questions of priority and route but also the standardization of design and construction and, where necessary, apportionment of cost.

It is, of course, mainly a long-term program, if only because road building, even by modern methods, is a lengthy operation. But agreement on which are the most pressing needs seems to ensure that this side of EEC activities will not face the same impasse that frustrates the complete integration of Western Europe.

JOINT EUROPEAN NUCLEAR TECHNOLOGY [6]

For a decade, Western Europe's first joint effort to develop a new technology has been quietly at work.

Now its engineers have an outstanding success to report.

They've developed a nuclear reactor that promises the cheapest atomic power yet made.

They've patented reactor inventions that could earn enough royalties to pay back the £31 million ($74.4 million) invested in the program by the twelve-nation partnership that backs it.

These are the tangible fruits of Project Dragon. The intangible gains may be just as significant.

In spite of Gaullism, monetary crises, and two renegotiations of the project agreement, Dragon has moved steadily toward its present success. It has proved that Europe can sink its rivalries in the interest of building up its technological strength as a whole.

[6] From article "Technology Plus: Joint European Research Develops Cheaper A-Plant," by Robert C. Cowen, natural science editor. *Christian Science Monitor.* p 12. Jl. 3, '69. Reprinted by permission from *The Christian Science Monitor.* © 1969 The Christian Science Publishing Society. All rights reserved.

Certainly project members are as proud of this as of their engineering triumph. They talked of it enthusiastically during their recent tenth anniversary celebration. Their *esprit de corps* flashed gaily in neckties, cufflinks, and lapel badges sporting the jaunty winged creature that symbolizes their joint efforts. . . .

Organized within the OECD (Organization for Economic Cooperation and Development), Dragon has enabled Europe to keep up with atomic-power developments that would otherwise leave many European countries behind.

Potential Savings Clear

It has been working on what engineers call a high-temperature, gas-cooled reactor. In terms of what it costs to build power stations or what you pay for electricity, that technical designation means potential savings.

In atomic power plants, a cooling fluid such as water or carbon dioxide gas carries off the heat of the nuclear "fire." This heat raises steam which then powers the turbines of electric generators. The hotter the coolant and the resultant steam, the more efficient is the generating process. So one way to bring down power costs is to boost operating temperatures.

To push these much above the few hundred degrees centigrade of present atomic plants, a coolant like helium gas has the edge. It's easier to handle than high-temperature liquids like sodium, which could be used. And, being a gas, it could run the turbines directly. This would get rid of the steam generators which boost power plant cost and waste heat.

Engineers knew all this in the mid-1950s. Some of them also foresaw that such plants might come into their own as nuclear technology matured in the 1970s. They also knew it would take an expensive development effort to get materials and reactor designs to stand up to high-temperature operation.

Few Could Afford It

The United States could afford this. So could a few European countries like Germany or Britain. But what could Norway, Switzerland, or Italy do? Even in those days, when atomic power was in its infancy, such countries could see themselves slipping behind in the technology of the future.

So Austria, Britain, Denmark, Norway, and Switzerland joined with the Euratom countries—Belgium, France, Germany, Italy, Luxembourg, and the Netherlands. They launched Dragon . . . on a beautiful heathland site provided by Britain on April 1, 1959. A decade later, their faith in this venture has paid off.

The Dragon reactor itself is just a test bed. It makes no electricity. Engineers throw away its 20 megawatts (20 million watts) of heat. But Dragon chief executive Dr. L. R. Shepherd has estimates showing the Dragon design could be scaled up to make cheap power.

He says a plant making 1,260 megawatts of electricity would cost about $120 a megawatt to build. It would make electricity for about 3.6 mils (0.36 cents) a kilowatt hour.

Britain's situation illustrates this. A 1,260-megawatt station built for $120 a megawatt would cost only two thirds to three quarters as much as one of the late-model atomic plants now being built. Moreover, Britain's newest atomic stations will undercut the cost of electricity from coal-, oil-, or gas-fired plants. . . .

Such a station would run with cooling-gas temperatures around 800° C. It would use conventional steam generators. However, Dragon engineers envision models running at 1,000° C and above, with the hot helium running the turbines directly. This kind of plant . . . would cut power costs by a further 5 to 25 per cent.

Partners Urged to Hurry

This money-saving technology has already been developed and proved out to the point where project member countries could begin building steam-generating plants. . . .

The United States is ready to market its own model gas-cooled reactor. A 40-megawatt prototype has been running at Peachbottom, Pennsylvania. . . . The designer, Gulf General Atomic, is to build a 330-megawatt power station in Platteville, Colorado.

Germany, too, is moving ahead. Besides sharing in Dragon, it has developed a gas-cooled reactor of its own. A 15-megawatt model has been tested at Jülich. A 300-megawatt power station may be under construction in North Rhine-Westphalia by January [1970].

Dragon members can cash in on their project in three ways.

They may share royalties from Dragon patents.

They have gained the know-how to build advanced power stations that could cut electricity costs at home.

And they could use that know-how to bid for contracts in power-station construction abroad. Dragon experts will work confidentially with individual companies in member countries to help them compete for such business.

All of this makes Dragon the first multinational development project in Europe to show a clear return to the partners for the money invested.

III. A EUROPE OF NATIONS

EDITOR'S INTRODUCTION

Despite the economic integration which has occurred in the past decade, Western Europe is still composed of highly individualistic nations that have no intention of submerging their identity in a supranational union. This section, therefore, attempts to portray several of the various countries in terms of some of the major concerns with which they are occupied and which will demand a large share of their attention in the near future.

The first article examines the current constitutional and political background in France and asks what will happen to the well articulated Gaullist policies without the leadership of de Gaulle. The article also goes into considerable detail on several important subjects: the overhaul of an antiquated social system; the development of a more efficient industrial sector; a more equitable distribution of wealth; and the need for France to capture a larger share of the foreign market.

The second article turns to Britain and describes the characteristics and nature of Britain's long-term economic crisis. The author identifies several factors contributing to this crisis: government policy which suppressed growth potential; industrial obsolescence which has made Britain unable to compete with some of the more modern industrialized countries; inadequacies in the civil service and in management; labor unions which demanded and received periodic pay increases in excess of increases in productivity. In the 1960s Britain began a serious attempt to remedy the defects through a plan for cooperative action by the government, industry, and unions. But the future of the British economy remains uncertain and no easy solution is at hand.

The following article turns to the export boom in Germany. This boom reflects the vigor of what is now one of the world's most powerful economies. There is every indication that the German economy will continue to surge ahead in the 1970s and increase its share of the export market.

The next article turns to Italy, which is being swiftly transformed by its industrial growth. A country of mass consumers is being created out of what had been largely a peasant society. Italy's economic expansion is the fastest in Europe and, globally, second only to that of Japan. The author uses the success of the Fiat automobile as a symbol of Italy's progress. But he also analyzes the Italian economy in terms of what has contributed to its strength.

The last article concerns Spain and describes the possible alternatives in the post-Franco era. In the middle of the 1960s, it appeared that Spain might be liberalizing its political institutions. This was largely an illusion. The regime's intentions toward democracy and reform, the author notes, were merely flirtatious.

AFTER DE GAULLE, A NEW DEAL FOR FRANCE'S ALLIES? [1]

Paradoxically, 1969 was the year in which the French paid tribute to one of their historic rulers while they got rid of another. Napoleon Bonaparte, born two centuries earlier, was commemorated from a safe distance. But the ever-present grandeur of Charles de Gaulle, founding father of the eleven-year-old Fifth Republic, had begun to grate on the nerves of France's voters. So last April [1969] they said *non* to their president's latest referendum—and found, somewhat to their surprise, that they had fired him.

After de Gaulle came no deluge—the chaos or communism he had often warned against—but instead what a London newspaper called a "deafening calm." The seventy-eight-year-old general quietly withdrew from center stage. And the reins of power passed smoothly to Georges Pompidou,

[1] From *Great Decisions 1970*. (Fact Sheet no 3) Foreign Policy Association. 345 E. 46th St. New York 10017. '70. p 27-37. Copyright 1970 by the Foreign Policy Association, Inc. Reprinted by permission.

his long-time political colleague, who was waiting in the wings.

Perhaps, as the New York *Times* has said, "the general's rule was so personal that it is a misnomer to talk of Gaullism without de Gaulle." Yet the Gaullist constitutional structure, the Gaullist bureaucracy and Gaullist politicians are presumably ensconced in power, at least until France's next parliamentary elections in 1973.

The big question, then, is: What will happen to Gaullist policies without de Gaulle? How much continuity in the direction of French affairs can we expect from the general's heirs? How much change?

To the rest of the world, and particularly to France's partners in the Western world, the course of French policy is of major concern. For the country's role is fundamental to the future of Western Europe and of the Western alliance.

Major Power, Strategic Ally

Geographically, France is not only the biggest country on the Continent but one of the most strategically situated. It is the most richly endowed by nature: if its soil were intensively cultivated, it could feed all of Western Europe. It ranks as the world's fifth richest nation in gross national product (GNP).

Politically and militarily, France has been demoted from its historic preeminence by the advent of nuclear superpowers and by the loss of its overseas empire. Even so, the country can still be classed as a "major" or "upper-middle" power. Its diplomatic expertise, industrial and technical skills, and cultural influence are held in wide esteem around the world—not least, in many former French colonies in Africa, Asia and the Middle East. The French conventional armed forces are large (over half a million regular personnel) and are supplied with first-rate equipment, much of it of wholly French design and manufacture.

France's nuclear *force de frappe* (strategic strike force) consists chiefly of atomic bombs and of twenty-seven intermediate-range ballistic missiles to be ready for service in 1971. Most experts consider the force too small to have substantial deterrent value against a major aggressor. But the country's prestige is probably served by its membership in the five-nation nuclear club.

The French have opted to retain their membership in the North Atlantic Treaty alliance, as distinct from the alliance's integrated military organization (NATO). They pulled out of the latter in 1966, obliging the NATO command to move its European headquarters from Paris to Brussels. Last year, on the twentieth anniversary of the North Atlantic Treaty, any member who wanted out could have given a year's notice of withdrawal; none of the fifteen members did.

To NATO planners, the collective defense of Western Europe would be virtually impossible without French cooperation. Thus, policy makers in NATO capitals, from Washington to Bonn, are alert for any signs of the new Pompidou government's intentions. How much military cooperation can the Western allies now count on from Paris? How much collaboration with NATO's long-range political goals of furthering East-West détente by moving "from peacekeeping to peacemaking," of becoming less of a "fort" and more of a "forum?"

Key to a United States of Europe

The other great issue between France and its partners may be of even more profound importance in the long run. This is the creation of a united Western Europe.

Without France, such a union is unthinkable. With France as a prime participant, there is reason to believe that the existing base, the six-nation European Economic Community (EEC), might one day be expanded and consolidated into a political federation of some kind. Eventually, all of Europe to its easternmost frontiers with Russia might assemble a vast array of national skills, resources, cultures and political systems into one great, sovereign confederation.

As of today, the twelve-year-old EEC is a successful customs union which has embarked on a few further ventures in economic cooperation. But progress toward genuine integration, beyond a common trade and agricultural policy, has been hampered in part by deep-rooted nationalist attitudes among the Six, in part by de Gaulle's intransigent opposition. And most observers hold de Gaulle primarily responsible for the fact that the club long refused to admit new members (Britain, Ireland, Denmark and Norway have all formally applied).

Now, with the general gone, will the French take fresh initiatives to construct a United States of Europe (whose chief architect is one of their own countrymen, Jean Monnet)? How far and how fast, if at all, will the Pompidou administration move to strengthen and enlarge the present EEC nucleus of France, West Germany, Italy, Belgium, Luxembourg and the Netherlands?

De Gaulle's Legacy

Of necessity, France's conduct abroad will be guided by conditions at home. Whether the country flourishes or falters domestically will largely determine the scope and success of its foreign policies.

In purely political terms, France has rarely looked healthier. If President Pompidou is not the universal choice of fifty million Frenchmen—he was elected by only 37 per cent of the registered voters—he nevertheless heads a solid majority regime. He was endorsed by a comfortable electoral margin over his presidential rivals. His political party dominates the National Assembly (lower house of parliament): nearly three quarters of the deputies represent the Gaullist Union of Democrats for the Republic . . . and the allied Independent Republicans. The cabinet, headed by Premier Jacques Chaban-Delmas, includes a number of non-Gaullists. But the coalition was formed by choice, to foster a broad national consensus, rather than dictated by political necessity.

All this presents a dramatic contrast to the Fourth Republic (1946-58), with its spinning carrousel of coalition governments—over two dozen in a dozen years. And much of the credit belongs to de Gaulle. He preferred to think of himself as a national rather than a political leader. Yet his greatest postwar contribution to his nation—after rescuing it from the colonial war in Algeria which had brought France itself to the brink of civil war—may prove to have been the creation of the first viable political majority in recent French history.

Many experts, however, insist on two qualifications to this achievement. One concerns the record of the much-maligned Fourth Republic. Despite the plethora of quarreling minority parties, the parade of what one commentator has called "so many clever, overeducated, feeble politicians" and the patched-together cabinets lasting a month or a year, there was remarkable continuity both in administration (by the able career civil service) and in national policy. From his Fourth Republic predecessors de Gaulle inherited a nation in agony over Algeria and troubled by a monetary crisis, but otherwise a going concern. By 1958 French economic recovery from World War II was complete. French industrial output was rising by an impressive 8 per cent a year. French statesmen had successfully piloted the project of European union through its initial stages: a coal and steel community, an atomic energy community and an infant Common Market or EEC.

Rejection of Arbitrary Rule

The other, more often cited qualification to de Gaulle's political achievement is that he carried stability too close to autocracy. . . .

Unlike Britain, the United States and several of the other Western democracies, France has tended to be a nation of politically unruly individualists who are more inclined toward critical opposition than civic participation, who expect more intellect than integrity from their leaders and whose political sympathies have often swung between libertarian and disciplinarian extremes.

De Gaulle did manage to weld much of the splintered French electorate in support of a strong, efficient and disciplined regime without sacrificing basic French liberties. What eroded his popular support, in the opinion of many commentators, was more his personal ruling style than the substance of his policies. His lofty manner and his increasingly arbitrary use of the powers entrusted to the president by the Fifth Republic Constitution gradually alienated millions of Frenchmen and helped to ignite the massive student and worker revolts of May and June 1968.

When the smoke cleared, however, French voters could see no alternative to the general except anarchy or communism. On June 30, 1968, they returned his party to parliament in a landslide. The Gaullist victory was engineered in large part by the tireless campaigning of the then Premier Pompidou—whom de Gaulle dismissed from his job soon afterward.

Subsequently, in January . . . [1969], Pompidou announced his availability for the presidency. To French voters, this meant that they now had a competent alternative to de Gaulle on hand. So, on April 27, 1969, they turned down a package referendum, part regional decentralization and part Senate reform, on which de Gaulle had mysteriously chosen to stake his own survival. With the president's immediate resignation, a celebrated career and a chapter in French history came to an end.

A Conservative Constituency

Now Pompidou has inherited the general's constituency. To some political analysts, this could mean a significant change in the country's political character. For France's voters have simultaneously rejected (1) the authoritarian style personified by de Gaulle; (2) the radical tradition perpetuated by the Communists and parts of the non-Communist left; and (3) the middle-of-the-roaders identified, rightly or wrongly, with the Fourth Republic's mediocre leadership. Instead, the long-fragmented electorate seems to have reached a fairly broad consensus—without precedent in recent history—in favor of "normalcy." ...

Much depends, of course, on how the new team responds to the challenges facing France. For the moment, at least, Pompidou and his colleagues have virtually no political competition to worry about. The only cohesive opposition party is the French Communist party, still the second largest in the West (after Italy's), but with a paltry 34 seats out of a total 487 in the Assembly. Only 90 deputies represent, among them, the various center and moderate-left parties of the Third and Fourth Republics. The impotence of these parties today is reflected as much by their internal divisions as by their failure to join forces in effective opposition to the Gaullists.

President, Cabinet, Parliament

Pompidou has also inherited a constitutional structure which in some ways more closely resembles the American presidential system than the parliamentary system of earlier French republics.

The French president is no longer a ceremonial figurehead chosen by a council of notables. He is a chief of state in fact, as well as name, elected by direct popular vote and empowered to appoint the government (i.e., the cabinet). The government, in turn, now enjoys prime responsibility for presenting new legislation to the National Assembly and deciding the agenda for debate. The Assembly does retain the power to topple the government by a majority vote of censure—but at the risk of having the president then dissolve the Assembly and decree new parliamentary elections.

De Gaulle, with his penchant for personal rule, designated several key areas of decision-making, notably foreign and military policy, as the "reserved domain" of the presidency. Whether the balance of authority among president, cabinet and parliament will remain as lopsided under his successor has yet to be seen. In practice, the distribution of powers may not matter too much as long as the French president has a solid working majority of his own party in the Assembly. But a tug of war between the president and a large parliamentary opposition, with the cabinet caught in the middle, could result in political paralysis and even a constitutional crisis.

New Wine in an Old Bottle?

With the new Gaullist leaders, French policy making has taken on a distinct new look. The preoccupation with prestige has given way to hard-headed pragmatism. Solitary decisions handed down from on high have yielded to *concertation*: the open exchange of information and ideas to encourage a consensus. The lonely figure of de Gaulle has been succeeded by a team of diverse personalities. . . .

By and large, the French appear to have little quarrel with the style—businesslike, accessible, informal—of their new leaders. But the success of Pompidou's "government of reconciliation" hinges, of course, on how effectively it performs.

How new is the wine in the familiar Gaullist bottle? Will the general's heirs create a new character for Gaullism, or will they stick closely to the founder's principles? Can they stick together as a cohesive political force without de Gaulle's commanding leadership? Or, as suggested by some recent incidents of disagreement among them, will the Gaullist movement now disintegrate into rival factions and personalities? At best, how long can it dominate the French political scene without effective opposition? And can the new government win the French public's wholehearted confidence and cooperation—both of which are indispensable to the improvement of the country's economy and social climate?

Priority on Home Improvement

In his first press conference after taking office, President Pompidou spelled out three priorities for his administration.

First, France must develop a more efficient and profitable industry, "the basis of any prosperity, hence, of any social progress."

Then, an equitable distribution of the national wealth throughout French society must be assured—specifically, through government action to redress the disadvantages suffered by certain social groups from "the necessary, the indispensable, transformation of our economy."

Finally, the French economy must be given an international dimension. French firms, "either by themselves or most often by agreement with other European and even non-European firms," must be equipped to compete in all the world's markets.

An Unbalanced Society

France today is at once strong and weak; alongside prosperity and political stability are economic hardship and social inequity, often rooted in outmoded institutions. A study by the country's respected General Planning Commission reached this frank conclusion: If France is to become a genuinely modern nation, nothing less than a complete overhaul of its educational system, its agricultural structure, its scientific research policies, its social security system and the management of its nationalized industries is called for. Moreover, public opinion polls have revealed a growing sensitivity among Frenchmen to their country's relative "backwardness" among the advanced nations.

The imbalances are striking. In a single metropolitan region, Paris, about a fifth of the population and nearly a quarter of the national income are concentrated, while some other regions of the country are badly underpopulated and economically depressed. About a tenth of all Frenchmen still live on the land. The proportion is dwindling but remains rather high for an industrialized country, since there are in fact "two agricultures": (1) a modern sector of large, mechanized, efficient and highly profitable farms; and (2) an antiquated sector of small, inefficient, unremunerative family holdings.

One reason the latter persists is because French law allows each one of a farmer's sons to inherit a share of the property. This encourages the progressive division of family property into many small, unproductive parcels. Another reason is the structure of guaranteed farm prices erected by the government over the years. Thus, farms otherwise incapable of independent survival are kept alive by whopping state subsidies (over 10 per cent of the 1969 national budget) while France is plagued by whopping farm surpluses, particularly of butter, milk, wheat and other cereals.

Other declining sectors of the French economy, such as coal and railways, are also heavily dependent on government subsidies. (What the state spends to cover the deficit of the French national railroad amounts to three times what it invests in new highway construction.)

Furthermore, many of France's basic industries (mechanical, electrical, chemical) are far less productive and profitable than some of their foreign competitors. Prices of some items run as high as 20 per cent above those for West German products, with a consequent loss of French export business to German manufacturers.

Labor Unrest

Despite these and other handicaps, most French industry is working at full capacity . . . with virtually full employment. There is actually a shortage of labor for many skilled jobs and a need for imported workers (some three million from North Africa, Spain and Portugal). Industrial wage increases have, by and large, kept abreast or ahead of rising prices. A substantial across-the-board raise, plus other benefits, was awarded in the wake of the massive strikes of May 1968, when at least seven million French workers (over a third of the labor force) walked off the job.

Yet unrest is chronic in labor ranks. Most commentators agree that this now poses the greatest single threat to the Pompidou government.

For one thing, workers in France's important public sector—all utilities and a number of other key industries are nationalized—have fared far less well than their counterparts in private industry. For another, France's affluent consumer society has whetted the wage-earner's appetite for a bigger slice of the pie.

French union leaders have claimed that the spring 1968 wage settlement was soon wiped out by cost-of-living increases. Their current wage demands, particularly those set forth by Georges Séguy, the Communist party official who heads the powerful General Confederation of Labor, are also motivated in part by an effort to regain control of the union rank and file. The latter staged the great wildcat strikes of 1968 without even consulting their chiefs, and have yet to be brought firmly back into line.

Social Attitudes and Alienation

Labor agitation is also a symptom of another imbalance in French society: the class structure.

Despite the hallowed commitment to *égalité* and *fraternité*, there is still too little mobility, too much suspicion among the country's various groups. The sociologist Michel Crozier, among others, has deplored the narrow social base of the French elites and the persistent barriers of class consciousness between workers and employers, between blue- and white-collar workers, between small tradesmen and large industrialists, etc. In principle, any qualified student is eligible for a higher education at little or no cost. In practice, few children from working-class families ever get to a university. Only a minority attend the academic high schools (*lycées*) to prepare for the baccalaureate certificate which is almost indispensable to a business or civil service career.

For this reason, the spectacle of some workers and university students joined in informal alliance during the May

1968 uprising was an extraordinary one. How could the factory proletariat make common cause—even temporarily—with the privileged offspring of the bourgeoisie?

According to many observers, both groups shared a sense of bitter alienation from the institutions that governed their lives. The workers felt that their interests were being ignored by their employers, their government and their union bosses alike. The students felt estranged from a centralized school system whose hidebound administration, crowded facilities and outdated curriculum seemed ill suited to prepare them for their roles in late twentieth century life.

The educational reform bill of late 1968 drafted by Edgar Faure, then minister of education, was a compromise effort—too radical for some tastes, too conservative for others—to decentralize and update the whole state-run university system. While the reform is being given a chance to take effect, the French campuses have been relatively quiet. But the French trade unions have not, as shown by a flurry of strikes beginning last September [1969]. Nor is much peace and quiet expected on the labor front while the Pompidou government tackles its most pressing task: what Giscard [Finance Minister Valéry Giscard d'Estaing] calls "disinflation" of the French economy.

An Illness of the Affluent

In one French official's metaphor, "France is an artificially drugged patient. She feels fine. Yet little by little she is being drained of all her blood."

Translation: French industry, except for a few declining sectors, is steaming along at full capacity. Factory order books are filled up; inventories are kept low; sales volume is limited only by the availability of production equipment and labor. But—and this is its basic ailment—French industry still cannot satisfy the voracious appetite of the French consumer market.

One inevitable result has been price inflation. Another, far graver in the long run, is a trade deficit. In an effort to keep up with domestic demand, France has been spending too much on imports and earning too little from exports; a sizable share of French output which would normally be sold abroad has been diverted to the home market.

In the first six months of 1969, for example, overall foreign trade amounted to almost a third more than the total for the same period in 1968. But while imports were 36 per cent higher, exports rose by only 27 per cent, and France's reserves of gold and foreign exchange drained out of the country during the first half of 1969. By June 30, reserves had dropped to $3.6 billion. If the hemorrhage continued the country would eventually be bled white of its capacity to buy and sell abroad.

As a corollary, France's own currency was ailing. De Gaulle had taken justifiable pride in having restored strength and stability to the franc. But over the past couple of years, particularly after the "inflationary" wage settlement of June 1968, both French and foreign businessmen lost confidence in French money and began converting their holdings into West German marks, Swiss francs and dollars. By November 1968 speculation against the "overvalued" French franc, in favor of the "undervalued" Deutsche mark, reached crisis proportions. However, de Gaulle adamantly refused to devalue. So an emergency $2 billion loan to Paris from the world's major financial capitals was required to stem the tide of speculation against the franc and to spare the international monetary system from convulsion.

Giscard's Prescription: Cool It

When Pompidou took office last June, the basic challenge facing his economic experts was how to lower France's inflationary fever without chilling the patient to death or provoking dangerous side effects (such as large-scale unemployment) .

After weighing alternatives, Finance Minister Giscard decided on a moderate course of treatment: Slow down domestic demand by inducing French consumers to spend less and save more, while simultaneously restoring the French franc to a sound international footing.

The expected benefits would be multiple. The price-wage spiral would be checked. The demand for imports would slacken while a bigger share of French production could be shifted to the export market, gradually restoring a healthy trade balance. This in turn would strengthen France's foreign-exchange reserves and help to stabilize its currency. Heavier saving would permit heavier investment in new techniques to make French industry more efficient, more profitable and more competitive on world markets.

Giscard's first specific step was a 12.5 per cent devaluation of the franc in August 1969 (from a little over U.S. $.20 to $.18). The adjustment was intended to be (1) modest enough to avert a chain reaction in the values of other currencies, which proved to be the case; yet (2) marked enough to discourage Frenchmen from buying imported goods and to attract foreigners with lower-priced French products. The hope, of course, was that French businessmen would not immediately nullify the devaluation by raising their export prices a commensurate 12.5 per cent.

Further cooling medicine was prescribed in the austerity program introduced by the government last fall. The French government itself would set a frugal example through substantial cuts in state expenditures, with a balanced budget promised for 1970. Various incentives, ranging from higher interest rates on bank savings to restrictions on consumer credit, were put forth to curtail private spending. (However, a tax increase was deliberately rejected. France—together with Sweden, also a welfare state with many nationalized enterprises—already bears the heaviest tax burden on the Continent.) And the government urged all Frenchmen to cooperate in the effort to restrain price and wage increases. For without such restraint the entire "disinflation" campaign would collapse.

Will the Treatment Work?

. . . The prospects for a successful cure for France's ailing economy . . . [are] far from clear. Critics and skeptics voiced a number of strong doubts about the government's course of therapy.

Since the 12.5 per cent devaluation only confirmed, officially, a loss of value which had already largely occurred in fact, how can it be expected to restore confidence in the franc? Is it possible to hold down domestic prices without, as a Toulouse merchant put it, stationing a gendarme in front of every display window in France? How can personal consumption be curbed when wage raises already outpaced price raises in 1969 and the unions are angrily demanding bigger benefits? How can government spending be slashed without provoking acute suffering, even a social upheaval, among the country's least prosperous groups—public-service employees, subsidized farmers, schoolteachers, pensioners, etc.?

And not least debatable, how strong a brake can the French afford to apply to their own economic boom, and to their imports from abroad, while their chief trading partners are caught up in the same "euphoria of expansion?" Giscard himself has acknowledged the need for moderation to avoid penalizing other countries: "If France no longer comes down with the flu when the United States sneezes, she is nevertheless no longer able, in the current free-trade atmosphere, to go on a strict austerity diet when others prefer to banquet."

The International Implications

Obviously, the heavy interdependence between France and its biggest trading partners—West Germany, Belgium and Luxembourg, Italy, the United States and the Netherlands, in that order—means that France's economic difficulties have an impact well beyond its own borders. The situation raises some disturbing issues.

In 1968, for example, France ran a trade deficit with every one of its five Common Market partners (total for the five: $1.2 billion) as well as with the United States (over $235 million). If this lopsided exchange continues, will it seriously impair France's role as a pillar of the EEC and a power in Europe? On the other hand, our manufacturers and farmers will be hurt if the French, to redress their trade balance, impose curbs on their imports from us. Will we not be tempted to retaliate with curbs on our imports from them, thereby undermining the whole French recovery effort?

Another issue turns on France's currency troubles. The United States and West Germany are the two governments which have dug deepest into their own treasuries to rescue the franc, both by direct loans to Paris and by making credits available through the International Monetary Fund. New international monetary arrangements—the use of "paper gold" and Eurodollars, for example—and West Germany's revaluation of its currency by slightly more than 9 per cent in October 1969 have helped to ease pressure on the franc and to bring greater stability to world money markets generally. Yet the long "gold war" waged by de Gaulle against the United States Treasury (the general repeatedly converted France's surplus dollars into gold at a time when the United States was struggling to halt a serious drain of its gold reserves) is still keen in Washington's memory.

In a larger sense, the weakness of the franc and the strength of the Deutsche mark tend to reinforce West Germany's economic predominance on the Continent. And this, in turn, raises the issue of West Germany's future role in the EEC. Are France's economic shortcomings serving to promote West German supremacy? If so, where will this lead?

West Germany is the richest and the most populous nation of Europe. Yet in their bilateral dealings with France and in EEC councils, the West Germans have usually adjusted their policies to French interests, for reasons stemming from past wars and the present division of Germany. However, as long as France fails to overcome its weaknesses and remains a junior economic partner, the West Germans are in fact the "more equal" in the relationship. Is it logical, and fair, to expect them to continue subordinating the realities of economic power to the diplomatic image of Franco-German harmony? Will Bonn's . . . Social Democratic chancellor, Willy Brandt, defer to President Pompidou as two of his predecessors, Chancellors Konrad Adenauer and Ludwig Erhard, deferred to de Gaulle? What new political patterns may emerge in Europe from the economic realities which now confront the French and their neighbors?

THE DILEMMAS OF THE BRITISH ECONOMY [2]

Britain's world position has been strongly affected in recent years by the chronic weakness of its economy. No government, Conservative or Labour, has managed to emerge from the cloud of economic crisis for any substantial length of time, with the result that the nation's dependence upon the actions of other nations, and on the international economy, has been frequently underlined. This does not mean that Britain is a poor country—it is still extraordinarily prosperous when compared with the developing countries, or even most of Europe. It does mean that the British have become increasingly sensitive to the contrast between what they once were as an economic power and their situation today, and to the contrast between what they would like to be and what they can probably afford. Thus the debate over the goals of the country is often tempered by the cold fact of its uncertain resources.

The examination of recent British economic problems can be divided roughly into two periods: 1950-61 and 1961-67. What distinguishes the two periods is not so much the character of the difficulties encountered—the slow rate of growth, the threat to the pound, the imbalance between imports and exports—as the way Britons have conceived and responded to them. In the earlier period the key word was stability: stability of employment, of the balance of pay-

[2] From *Britain at the Crossroads*, pamphlet by J. B. Christoph, professor of government at Indiana University. (Headline Series no 186) Foreign Policy Association. 345 E. 46th St. New York 10017. '67. p 16-29. Copyright 1967 by Foreign Policy Association, Inc. Reprinted by permission.

ments, of labor-management relations. Since 1961 the pressures for stability have remained strong, but they have been supplemented, and occasionally replaced, by pressures for growth and reform. If words can sum up attitudes, it is revealing that Britons in the fifties talked mainly about the "management" of the economy, whereas in the sixties they have talked more about its "planning." The thrust toward modernization that is being felt in other parts of British life is now affecting the economy, with results which are still mixed and hard to judge, but of striking importance.

What kinds of economic conditions did British leaders in the sixties inherit from the preceding decade? Perhaps the most striking of them was the sluggishness of Britain's rate of growth, especially when compared to that of its European neighbors. For some years these important differences were not recognized or digested, being attributed to simply "catching up" on the part of countries (like France) whose growth in the interwar years was microscopic, or to special situations, as in Germany, which had been forced to rebuild its productive capacity from scratch and which did not share Britain's heavy military expenditures. But when these developments continued into the second half of the fifties, it became increasingly apparent that there was more wrong with Britain's performance than could be explained away by the peculiarities of other countries' circumstances. By prewar standards British growth was quite respectable, but for an exporting nation in a highly competitive international economy, it was disquieting.

Nor do the statistics bear out the charge that the level of British taxes and welfare programs was dampening initiative and thus impairing growth. British direct and indirect taxes took up about one fourth of the gross national product, just about the same proportion as in every other industrial country in Western Europe. Its expenditures on social security and allied programs accounted, in fact, for a smaller proportion of national income than in France, Germany and Italy, and for about the same as in Sweden and Holland. Its military spending did account for a somewhat larger proportion of national income than its European neighbors, but the figure is not large enough to explain differences in performance. There are two more plausible explanations for Britain's slow growth. The first is that British governments in their preoccupation with stability had followed policies which suppressed the growth potential of the economy. The second is that the very structure of British industry had become outdated and thus incapable of achieving the level of productivity required for competitive survival. A brief look at the practices of the fifties will bear out the validity of these explanations.

Stop-and-Go

The return to power of the Conservatives in 1951 was followed by a rapid dismantling of the direct controls imposed by the Labour government immediately after the war. The basic principle was the reassertion of market forces loosely guided by anticyclical . . . policies on the part of the government. The chief task of government was seen as one of stabilizing conditions by alternately stimulating and restraining the level of economic activity. The zigzag pattern followed in these years was popularly known as "stop-and-go," resulting from a deliberate policy of priming the pump or applying the brake as threats occurred. To do this, the government had at its disposal a number of indirect weapons: for example, the power to raise or lower taxes, to change the bank rate (the British equivalent of the Federal Reserve discount rate, which influences the ease or difficulty of borrowing), to set restrictions on credit buying, and so forth. None of this should strike the American reader as unfamiliar. What was different was the frequency and speed with which stop became go and then stop again. The timing of these fiscal and monetary changes was such as to keep British industry in a state of great uncertainty, and long-range growth plans could not be developed with any confidence. Had these policies worked, they might have been justified as a rational choice between difficult goals. But on the whole they did not succeed in achieving the stability that was intended, and British industry seemed to be getting the worst of both possible worlds.

The situation was complicated by Britain's unsatisfactory balance-of-payments position. Throughout this period its volume of imports always exceeded its exports, and revenue earned from "invisible" sources (tourism, banking, shipping, insurance, etc.) —which in prewar years had been an enormous cushion—was now insufficient to make up the gap. As a result Britain's low financial reserves dwindled even further, and loans from other countries or international agencies had to be sought from time to time. Without satisfactory reserves to back it up, sterling as an international currency came under constant pressure. To stave off a run on the pound, British governments were forced to dampen down the domestic economy by various restrictive measures. Here we have one of the great dilemmas of postwar British economic policy. An interlude of expanding demand and growth requires a rising level of imports, which is likely to cause an imbalance in Britain's international payments, which in turn induces the government to tighten up credit and restrain demand. Productivity declines. Noting this, the government responds by loosening credit and stimulating demand, and the cycle is complete. . . .

The responsibility for the unsatisfactory working of the economy cannot be laid entirely to the policies followed by governments in the fifties. It can be attributed equally to the attitudes and practices of those in a position to do something about the state of production. Critics never tire of jabbing at three groups in particular—the civil service, industrial management and the trade unions. These proved to be fashionable scapegoats, and their complacency invited criticism and disapproval.

Weaknesses of the Economy

Considering the great power exercised by British governments over the economy in the postwar period, it is not surprising that Britons came to worry over the qualities of the civil servants who advised the laymen charged with political responsibility for the big decisions. Much was made of the fact that most of the senior civil servants were "amateurs," making key judgments on the fate of the economy, but by background and habits isolated from the real world of industrial production, modern management and labor relations. Most of them were Oxford or Cambridge graduates trained in classical subjects whose style of living was remote from the daily problems of the mines, mills and chemical works. Nor were there professionals even in the field of economics. During the fifties, for instance, the civil service as a whole employed less than a dozen professional economists, and in the most important ministry handling economic problems, the Treasury, the key posts were solidly in the hands of the amateurs. Under these circumstances, critics argued, the old tradition of defending the pound at almost any price inevitably prevailed, and progressive businessmen and growth-minded economists had difficulty getting a hearing. Before the economy could be modernized, it was said, the civil service would have to come into the light of the real Britain.

The going standard of industrial management was also not without weaknesses. British industrialists showed themselves to be slow in embracing commercial and technological changes that were sweeping Europe and America. There were progressive and enlightened firms (mainly the bigger ones), and British laboratories produced some notable innovations. But the smugness and caution that was rampant in the civil service also characterized much of industry. Top management was often cool to professional and scientific talent and preferred training in classics and letters to engineering. Down to the sixties there was not a single school of business administration or management studies in Britain. One learned the job in the age-old way, which tended to perpetuate age-old ideas and techniques. British products, many of superior quality, ran into difficulties on the world market, not only because of the higher labor costs incurred in making them, but also because of unaggressive salesmanship, delays in delivery and servicing snags. Finally, management's relations with labor tended to be distant and aloof, and while Britain suffered fewer strikes than many other countries, the strikes it had pinched harder, and industrial relations were honeycombed with restrictive practices on both sides. In the climate of stop-and-go, industrial peace was often valued over programs to increase productivity.

The British workingman did very well for himself in the fifties. Unemployment levels seldom exceeded 2 per cent nationally (though the figure was higher in Scotland, Northern Ireland and northeast England), and wages advanced smartly on most fronts, keeping well ahead of rising living costs. In the period 1950-60 production per capita grew in Germany at the rate of 6.5 per cent; in Italy, 5.3 per cent; and in France, 3.5 per cent. The British figure was 2.2 per cent. The British found it difficult to use labor to maximum advantage. Many of the conservative and restrictive attitudes displayed by management were also found on the labor side. Memories of the bad old days—the unemployment and breadlines of the thirties—were still alive in the minds of labor leaders, who were determined to spread the work in such a way that every worker could be assured of a secure job. Most shops suffered from various kinds of restrictive practices, and there was often resistance to the introduction of labor-saving machinery and newer methods. The government was increasingly expected to enter industrial conflicts as referee or briber. In the fifties, when labor was in short supply, many employers went along with wage demands without asking for an equivalent rise in productivity and even hoarded labor for fear of being left behind when the government gave the next green light to the economy. The British worker, who after years of struggle now was enjoying a spell of prosperity, was really in no mood to see his wages tied strictly to increased productivity.

Here we must mention one of the apparent puzzles of British life in the past fifteen years: the contrast between the fragile condition of the national economy and the visible affluence of Britons in their daily lives. At the very time that the country's balance of payments has shown continuous deficits, its share of world trade declining and its productivity lagging behind neighboring nations, the British consumer has been doing quite well for himself. Since 1951 the ownership of cars has increased fourfold. Former luxuries, like refrigerators, washing machines and continental holidays, now are the natural expectations of the middle class and much of the working class. Nine out of ten British homes have TV; even central heating is gaining in popularity. Supermarkets offering a wide range of goods are now in every neighborhood, with the usual effect on independent merchants. In sharing the same consuming habits and leisure activities the classes have become closer than they have ever been. And though important pockets of poverty remain—especially in the depressed regions of the north and among older people on pensions—they are both less severe and less visible than before the war.

The connection between this rising standard of consumption and the persistence of national economic crisis is complex and cannot be summed up in a few words. An improvement in one does not bring an automatic improvement in the other; and under certain conditions—as when a company has a choice of producing for the booming domestic market rather than the tougher export market—one may in fact suffer because of progress in the other.

Pressure for Reform

The picture has been changing markedly in the last half dozen years. At just about the time the British awoke to the potentialities of entering the Common Market, they also began to view their economic institutions in a different light, with the result that official policy and private thinking

are far different from ten years ago. The changes can be
dated from the year 1961, when the Macmillan government
moved cautiously away from the old formulas. Several forces
converged to work shifts in basic attitudes. One was growing
pressure from business groups, especially the Confederation
of British Industry, for something more predictable to replace the zigzag policies that had dominated the fifties. Another was the rising influence of politicians and civil servants
who believed that the time was ripe for Britain to adopt the
kind of planning that they saw as responsible for France's
economic successes. (This was part of the larger "rediscovery
of Europe" going on in the early sixties.) Finally, under increasing fire after ten years in office, the Conservatives were
anxious to show that they were still capable of fresh action
in key areas of public concern. Clearly the economy was more
than ready for a "new look."

"Indicative Planning"

The main element of the new policy was the notion of
"indicative planning." It involved not a shift in ownership
but a new concept of shared responsibility for economic
growth on the part of the government, industry and the
unions. The old fairly rigid frontier that had inhibited consultations between these groups was now erased. Henceforth
the big economic decisions were to be made jointly by all
three and brought together in the form of plans valid for
four or five years instead of month by month. On a voluntary
but authoritative basis the partners were to consult continu-
ously to make sure that their own projected plans—for capital investment, for manpower, for public expenditure—took
account of the plans of the others, and they were then to
coordinate their plans accordingly. It was hoped that this
new system, which depended largely on the goodwill and
patriotism of all, would overcome the obstacles to growth
so deeply imbedded in British economic life. Under the Conservatives little more occurred than the acceptance by organized industry and labor of a commitment to these new

procedures; but psychologically it was an important development in modern British history.

The planning mechanism developed by the Conservatives has changed considerably since Labour came to power in 1964, but the essence of the commitment remains. The shift from the earlier preoccupation with full employment and short-term demand management to a new accent on growth was symbolized by the downgrading of the Treasury and the establishment of a Ministry of Technology and a National Economic Development Council (NEDC, or "Neddy"), the latter outside the formal channels of administration. Neddy, created by the Conservatives in 1962, and later reorganized by Labour, brought together the most important economic ministers, employers' representatives and trade union leaders to hammer out the plans and communicate them to their colleagues. Modernization commissions were set up for major industries and staffed with experts who were to locate the chief impediments to growth and find ways to eliminate them. Most important, Neddy was given a small but high-powered central office, made up not of the usual civil service types, but of professionals from several walks of life—economists, scientists, statisticians, businessmen, engineers. Its example was contagious: other government departments made similar efforts to recruit this kind of talent, and amateurism is now on the wane in the civil service.

It may well be that such changes in attitude and personnel were the real accomplishments of the first years of the new economic policies. The five-year plan developed by Neddy and accepted by the government went rather badly awry after two years in operation. After some early success in reaching the target figure of a 4 per cent rate of growth per annum, the plan was upset by a new balance-of-payments crisis in 1964 and by the inability of Conservative governments to get an incomes policy that would keep wage increases in line with productivity.

Labour's version of indicative planning is not radically different from the Conservatives', but different in organiza-

tion and stress. Wilson has tightened up the planning structure by bringing it into the inner circle of government power,
essentially in his own hands. The heart of Neddy's operation
was transferred into a new Department of Economic Affairs,
headed first by the Labour party's number two man, George
Brown, and now by the prime minister himself. The party
has always been full of economists, and today not only does
a key group of them hold Cabinet posts, but a steady stream
of academic experts now moves in and out of government
to prescribe for the economy. Still, it is easier to proclaim
the need to modernize the economy than to bring this about,
and even with the changes wrought by Labour many of the
old intractable problems remain. The will has not always
produced the way.

Consider the fate of the National Plan, an omnibus
growth projection produced in Labour's first year in office.
It called for an increase in the national product of 25 per
cent between 1964 and 1970 (or an annual average of 3.8 per
cent, a shade less than the Conservatives' projection for 1961-
66). The outcome of lengthy exchanges between government,
industry and the unions, the plan assumed that Britain's
exports would rise above the level of imports, that funds for
expansion would be available in reasonable amounts and
that public expenditure would increase about 4 per cent annually in these years. Public hurrahs for the plan had hardly
subsided, however, when Britain was plunged into another
economic crisis. For the second time in two years the pound
weakened on the international market, the balance of payments worsened and inflationary pressures mounted. Confidence in Britain waned among the "gnomes of Zurich"—
British slang for international banking circles—and the Wilson government had to apply the brakes to dampen down
expansion at home. The bank rate went up to 7 per cent,
installment down payments were increased, cuts in public
spending announced and building controls applied. The
number of unemployed advanced and 1965 private productive investment had fallen by almost 10 per cent. For all its

good intentions, the Labour government had failed to surmount stop-and-go. . . .

Equally important, if less dramatic, are the changes occurring in the understructure of the British economy. The need to modernize, so slowly appreciated in the past, is now strongly felt, discussed and often acted upon. That portion of the civil service which deals with economic affairs, for example, is feeling the wind of change. From less than a dozen in the fifties, the number of working economists in the government has increased from thirty in 1964 to over one hundred in 1966. Recruits coming into the administrative class—the highest echelon of the civil service—now are required to take courses at the Center for Administrative Studies, organized in 1963. Amateurism within industry is declining. Employers and executives are now grouped in a single national association (the Confederation of British Industry), which is more professionally staffed than in the past and better served by statistical and computerized facilities. The government and a businessmen's fund have jointly established Britain's first schools of business in London, Manchester and Oxford. Expenditure on scientific and technological research more than doubled from 1955 to 1965 and now takes 2.6 per cent of the gross national product, the highest proportion in Europe. (The United States figure is 3.7 per cent.) Applied science is now better regarded, and facilities for adding to the short supply of scientists, engineers and technicians are increasing rapidly. The trade unions have been slower to move. Some of the bigger unions have begun to streamline their archaic structures and to consider ways to reduce the ridiculous number of unions employers have to deal with. With the help of government they have got employers to replace "on the job" apprenticeship with schemes for training or retraining workers in more advanced skills.

The future of the British economy remains uncertain. It is in transition, caught between the pressure on the one hand of old but persistent problems, traditional ways and conservative ideas and, on the other hand, of rapid change, new attitudes and different kinds of men. The experiment with planning has been significant psychologically though not a striking success in practice. Steps forward—toward better co-operation between government, industry and organized labor; toward an effective incomes and prices policy; toward reforms in the structures of production—continue to be hampered by the persistence of crisis and the small margin of error the British economy is allowed today. Many Britons are convinced that salvation will come only if the country enters the larger market of Europe. But others, observing the recent difficulties of the Common Market countries, are less sanguine about this prospect and argue that Britain must pull itself up by its own bootstraps. Quick cures are not on the horizon. There are bound to be difficult decisions ahead for those who direct the British economy.

GERMANY'S EXPORT BOOM [3]

The revaluation of the mark . . . [in October 1969] theoretically should take some of the steam out of West Germany's export boom—and, by extension, correct the nation's top-heavy balance of payments.

But German businessmen, who are almost as proud of the postwar recovery of their exports as of the "economic miracle" of prosperity itself, are anything but pessimistic about foreign sales. "Our rate of increase may slow," says . . . [a] foreign trade specialist at Hamburg's International Economics Institute, "but our export volume will continue to grow." And an official in the Economics Ministry sums up the government view urbanely: "The amount of the revaluation [a bit over 9 per cent] was not set so that we would lose our export markets."

Record. In the past twenty years, Germany has expanded exports about twelve times, to nearly $25 billion . . . [in 1968]. And for the past eighteen years the Germans have exported

[3] From "Germany's Export Boom Steams Right Ahead." *Business Week.* p 112-14+. N. 1, '69. Reprinted from the November 1, 1969 issue of *Business Week* by special permission. Copyrighted © 1969 by McGraw-Hill, Inc.

more than they have imported. In recent years, in fact, they have been rubbing it in by widening their surplus at a time when other major exporters, including the United States, are having their troubles with trade. . . .

[In 1969] German exporters continued their gains, despite the handicap of an ersatz revaluation in the form of a 4 per cent penalty on everything they shipped in the first nine months. Now, by all indications, the Germans expect to go right on with their dazzling display of expert salesmanship around the world. Although revaluation is supposed to make the nation's exporters less competitive, many of them proved with the 4 per cent export tax that they could absorb or pass along the added burden with hardly a ripple in their sales figures.

Some German goods stand to sell well even if their prices in world markets show the full effect of revaluation. Says an official of Germany's machine industry: "Capital goods aren't so price sensitive as consumer goods. When you sell a highly refined milling machine, for example, this usually involves custom tailoring which somebody has to have anyway." Machinery accounts for a fifth of German exports.

Other exporters say they are ready to absorb most of the revaluation themselves. Even if profits slide, says a spokesman for AEG-Telefunken, the big electrical equipment maker, exports must continue. "We simply cannot afford to lose markets that we developed with great effort and investment. These markets are crucial to our future development." Like many other German companies these days, AEG-Telefunken can afford to soak up higher costs. The company raised profits better than 20 per cent . . . [in 1968], to $40 million on sales of $1.3 billion.

Volkswagen does plan to raise its export prices from 7 per cent to 11 per cent, depending on the market. But in Britain, where VW figures higher prices could hurt sales, there will be no markups.

Impact. Actually, the cost increase for German exports was slightly more than had been expected, and it produced

some grumbling in industrial circles. Still, the overall outlook for foreign sales remains good. This year's export surplus is expected to be a robust $3.75 billion to $4 billion. This
week, the central bank, the Economics Ministry, and private
economists were speculating that if the trade surplus dropped
next year it would not be by much.

"Any shrinkage will likely be as much the result of cooling off in other economies as it will be of revaluation," pre-
dicts a government economist. In particular, Germany has an
eye on the United States.

A major reason for so much optimism is that, as Germany
and its competitors know full well, price plays only a supporting role in Germany's export extravaganza. More important
is that Germany is selling exactly the products—machinery,
vehicles, chemicals, iron and steel, and electrical equipment
—that are most in demand by the countries best able to pay
for them. And revaluation has no effect at all on the fabled
German workmanship or the ability of German companies to
deliver on time.

Selective. More than any other nation, Germany sells the
right things to the right people. At a time when the world is
hungry for machinery, for example, Germany has it to sell.
Says . . . [a] foreign trade specialist of the German Electro-
Technical Industry Association: "There is a world investment boom, and we have a lot of investment goods to offer.
And while the world was in this boom, Germany was coming
out of a recession [in 1967 and part of 1968] with a lot of
unused capacity. Naturally, we have profited."

Furthermore, Germany sells its classy line of capital goods
to the best customers in the world. While the United States
sends 30 per cent of its exports to developing nations, Germany puts far less emphasis on beating the bushes in South
America, Asia and Africa. Some 82 per cent of its exports goes
to the industrialized world. "Importing is a function of the
gross national product," says . . . [the Hamburg specialist
quoted above] "and we concentrate our exports on the
countries with the healthiest GNP's."

Meticulous. There is no single reason for the German ability to sell in these lucrative markets. But one answer that pops up often around the world is what the Germans delight in calling *Deutschewertarbeit,* or German quality workmanship.

In Japan, for example, German goods have a built-in reputation for quality that no amount of advertising could buy. Much of this is a hangover from World War II, when the two countries were allies and the Japanese developed a healthy respect for German goods in comparison to their own somewhat shabby products. But even today, when Japan makes a wide range of good-quality compact cars, affluent Japanese are ready to pay almost twice as much for a Volkswagen as for a comparable domestic car. And many Japanese professional photographers will pay a premium price for a Leica even while professionals in the rest of the world are switching to the made-in-Japan Nikon.

Half a world away, in Buenos Aires, an Argentinue government official swears by German quality: "Right after the war, the general quality of European goods coming into Argentina was bad. But from the very first minute, the Germans were producing top quality. A Mercedes-Benz imported in 1948 was even better than one bought in 1939."

Tender care. German exporters win a lot of points by delivering the goods on time. The director of a German engineering firm gloats: "We delivered a plant to an African country and put it down right on time. A high government official was rubbing his hands with glee. 'This is different from our usual experience,' he told us."

In large measure, on-time delivery is a consequence of having a fairly docile labor force. Strikes are uncommon. But the Germans make an effort to pamper their markets. The German word for this is *pflegen,* which translates as cultivate, tend, nurse, or cherish, and many German companies take all its meanings seriously. For example, when German exporters got into trouble with wildcat strikes in September, many sent out senior executives to explain the delays and estimate new delivery dates.

Germans say they take these pains because they have an "export mentality." And some of Germany's competitors agree. An official with a British trade organization says, "There is no mystique about exporting in Germany. To the German businessman, trade is trade whether it's at home or abroad."

Germans have been thinking this way since the nineteenth century. While Britain was selling mightily to a captive market of colonies around the world, empireless Germany had to scratch for exports among its demanding European neighbors. And German companies had to keep on scratching because the destruction and confiscations of two wars have reduced their overseas production capacity and forced them to rely almost entirely on exports to reach foreign markets.

Sales talent. The Germans are far from perfect at understanding their foreign customers. Among the hard-selling Japanese, they are criticized for failing to follow up sales. "The German policy is sell and forget about it," says a disgruntled official of a Japanese trading company. "We keep telling them they could sell more if they improved their marketing policy, but it does no good." And in Brazil, a shipment of German electric motors is marooned in an in-bond warehouse because it entered the country without the proper customs papers. Company lawyers are trying to put things right.

Such miscues are not common, however, because German companies put a lot of emphasis on training men for the export business. "A couple of years on the spot overseas is par for the course," says one German businessman. Another points out that German companies get much of their export talent from the German banks, whose executives are heavily involved in the financing of exports. "The banks build a reserve for the companies," says this official.

The Germans are also proud of their ability to speak the local language, although most admit that the Dutch take first prize in this department. Says Otto Meyer, general manager of Demag, the big machine producer: "I have a friend in Spain who is a representative for an American company. He says they always send him salesmen who only speak English. When I send a man out, the first thing I want to know is whether he speaks the language."

Demag's own example in exporting is impressive. The company was hit hard by the 1967 recession, which produced a domestic investment slump. Demag's German sales sagged 19 per cent. Going full blast after new foreign customers, Demag raised its exports 15 per cent above the average of the preceding five years and held its total sales drop for 1967 to 5 per cent.

Meyer now feels that Demag can counter the revaluation with similar flexibility. One tactic, he says, is to produce more in facilities outside Germany. Another is to push for more increases in productivity at home.

Bankrolling. With the bulk of German sales going to well-heeled industrial nations, financing is not a decisive sales tool. But the Germans are not limping in this field. German banks have had plenty of money to offer at easy rates, and the booming German companies themselves are well heeled. Says . . . a director of Schering, the big pharmaceuticals company: "The problem of the German company has not been one of getting money but of what to do with it."

Financing plays a big part in German export success in South America. In São Paulo, Brazil, the German company Hochtief recently captured a $17 million subway engineering contract by offering to take payment over five years, with a two-year grace period. In Argentina, ITT's Standard Electric went to the mat earlier this year with Germany's Siemens over a fat telephone equipment order from Entel, the government telecommunications company. When the dust settled, ITT had a $25 million chunk of the business and Siemens had $20 million. But ITT's original credit terms of 10 per cent or 11 per cent had been chewed down to 9 per cent with Siemen's offer of 8 per cent.

Says ITT's financial controls manager in Argentina . . . :
"The Germans aren't murdering us, but they are beginning
to hurt. The main difference is financing. On the Entel deal,
the Germans got their financing arranged in a week while we
had to hustle to do it in a month."

Long view. With all this going for them, few German
companies expect to be hurt badly by revaluation. And
Michalski, in a forthcoming book, *Exports and Economic
Growth,* argues that Germany has no choice but to become
an even bigger exporter.

A SOCIETY TRANSFORMED BY INDUSTRY [4]

In the land of Michelangelo, Garibaldi and the Medicis
there reigns a vast and unusual variety of contemporary
heroes. The Italians idolize Grand Prix drivers, artists, novel-
ists and occasionally Sicilian *banditti.* They fall barely short
of adoring Nino Benvenuti, the boxing champion. They
lavish attention on their celebrated movie directors—Anto-
nioni, Fellini, Rossellini. And who, of course, could overlook Gina or Sophia?

To this colorful collection the Italians have lately added
a less likely hero: the industrialist. He has earned national
popularity because he and his kind are transforming Italy.
The industrialists have produced an economic expansion
that Italians call *Il Miracolo* or, simply, *Il Boom,* which has
laced the countryside with crowded *autostrade* and studded
the cities and villages with TV antennas. More fundamentally, *Il Boom* is converting Italy from a peasant society that
served an élite into a consumer society that caters to the mass
of the country's 54 million people.

The most widely admired and envied Italian industrialist—the *Numero Uno*—is Giovanni Agnelli, the head of auto-
making Fiat. Turin-based Fiat, which has produced four
out of every five cars on Italy's roads, has done more than
any other Italian firm to shape the country's new affluence

[4] From article in *Time.* 93:58-62. Ja. 17, '69. Reprinted by permission from
Time, The Weekly Newsmagazine; Copyright Time Inc. 1969.

at home and influence abroad. "Agnelli has a mythology not unlike President Kennedy's," writes British journalist Anthony Sampson in *The New Europeans*. "Clearly his presence fills some kind of psychological gap." . . .

Fiat is more than a company; it is a city-state. Most of its 157,000 employees work in twenty-two plants around smog-covered Turin. Their paychecks, which average $1.28 an hour for a 45-hour week, directly support 40 per cent of the city's 1.3 million population. Fiat has company housing, company resorts and entertainment, company clinics and sports teams—but few company strikes. There have been work stoppages on only thirty-four days in the past six years. Fiat also controls Turin's *La Stampa* (circulation 500,000), which is probably Italy's best daily after the *Corriere della Sera*. It far outsells the Communist daily *L'Unita* among Turin's workers. Like Agnelli, the paper is undogmatic, progressive and slightly left of center on most issues.

The giant that Gianni Agnelli operates . . . had all-time-high sales [in 1968] of $2.1 billion. It turned out 1.75 million cars as well as turbines, jet fighter planes, trucks, diesel engines and farm equipment. For the second year in a row, Fiat out-produced Volkswagen (1,603,500 cars) and ranked as the biggest auto company outside the United States. Shipments abroad of Fiats, by far Italy's biggest export item, rose in 1968 from 398,000 cars to 535,000, worth $496 million. Even in Germany, home of the Volkswagen, 1 out of 13 cars is a Fiat. Sales to the United States have been relatively modest because Agnelli has concentrated on exports to Europe and has only recently begun a drive to market a broader range of bigger cars in America. Still, Fiat's U.S. sales doubled in 1968 to 31,000. . . .

[In November 1968], Fiat leaped further across national borders—and advanced the cause of European integration—by taking over France's Citroën. Agnelli personally negotiated the deal with some friends, France's tiremaking Michelin family, which controls Citroën. Agnelli sought an outright takeover, but Charles de Gaulle objected and the French government limited Fiat to a 15 per cent holding in the firm. In fact, Fiat will get effective control of Citroën through a complex holding-company arrangement."Have no doubts about it," Agnelli told a friend. "The merger is complete." When the Fiat-Citroën "collaboration" formally begins . . . [in January 1969], Agnelli will, in effect, preside over a combine with total sales of $3 billion and annual production of more than two million cars.

Agnelli is also looking to Eastern Europe, where the auto market is underdeveloped and potentially great. Tito's Yugoslavia builds Fiats under a licensing arrangement, and Poland recently signed a similar agreement to build "Polski-Fiats." Russia has hired Fiat to help it construct and run an $800-million plant at Togliattigrad on the Volga. The huge plant is scheduled to begin producing Fiats by early 1970, and work up to an annual output of 600,000. . . .

If Agnelli is not exactly typical of Italy's industrialists, he is certainly foremost among them. Like Italian architects, film makers and sculptors, Italian industrialists have a certain flair. In the board room as on the opera stage Italy is a nation of soloists; committee rule is rare, and stock ownership has not yet diminished the powers of owners and operators. Their accomplishments are all the more remarkable because the country is poor in resources, save for the ingenuity, inventiveness and individualism of its managers.

There is practically no oil in Italy, yet the state-run . . . monopoly became a world petroleum power under the late Enrico Mattei and his successor, Eugenio Cefis. Mattei bought crude from the Soviets, developed natural-gas resources in the Po Valley, and proudly declared that in building . . . [the oil industry], "I broke 8,000 laws." To sidestep Cyclopean bureaucrats—with their time-consuming rules about building permits and their endless paper work—he laid the pipelines at night, while the officials slept.

Italy also has very little coal or iron. When, in 1947, some Italian leaders requested a World Bank loan to build a steel industry, the bankers rather snidely advised them to stick to growing tomatoes. But industrialist Oscar Sinigaglia, then head of the state-owned Finsider steel complex, landed a big order from Fiat and went on to locate his mills at ports, where ships bring in coal and steel from the cheapest foreign sellers. Finsider is now Europe's biggest steel producer, and last year Italy's output rose from 17.4 million tons to 18.7 million, fifth highest in the world.

In other fields, Olivetti's business machines are known the world over. Pirelli exports tires to more than one hundred countries, and has become the Continent's biggest tire company. In publishing, Milan's Fabbri Brothers created a major business by capitalizing on Italy's rising educational levels and its fascination with installment-plan buying. They brought out high-quality serializations of *The Divine Comedy,* the Bible and other works [which] now sell more than one million copies a week on Italian newsstands. Italian designers are famed for what they do with silks and leather, and their fashions are in high demand. French, Dutch and Belgian appliance firms have been unable to compete with lower-priced Italian refrigerators and washing machines. Italian construction combines outbid competitors for huge jobs in Africa, Latin America and Asia. Says a Milan-based builder: "Being a bit of an underdeveloped country yourself helps you work in other underdeveloped regions."

Europe's Fastest-Moving Economy

Powered by industry, Italy's economic expansion has been the fastest in Europe and second in the world only to Japan's. In the past three years, production of goods and services has risen an average 5 per cent a year, to $72 billion in 1968, and is expected by the European Economic Commission to gain another 6 per cent this year. It is true that Italy is growing fast partly because it has considerable catching up to do; Italy's economy remains one twelfth as big as the U.S.'s economy and half the size of West Germany's.

Yet few countries have a stronger trading position in world markets. The increasing shipments of Italian steel, refrigerators, TV sets, typewriters, tires—and cars—have lifted exports by almost 200 per cent since 1960, to 1968's $10 billion. Italy had a comfortable $600 million surplus in its balance of payments for 1968, when its reserves of gold and currency exchange rose to $5.2 billion, a total exceeded only by the United States and Germany. The Italian lira ranks with the German mark as one of the world's soundest currencies, and it is eagerly sought by speculators, who bet on its upward revaluation in the not-distant future. A grudging testimonial to its strength came . . . when the United States Treasury, in a report on the American balance of payments problem, suggested that the defense of the dollar would be easier if Italy and West Germany did not promote exports quite so aggressively.

Though the country's export success is partly due to the relatively low wages of its workers, prosperity has spread fairly widely among the people. Per capita income has doubled in a decade to $1,340 a year. In a country where even ice cubes were scarce a decade ago, 65 per cent of the families now have refrigerators. About 40 per cent own washing machines, and 60 per cent heat their frozen pizza in gas or electric ovens.

The most conspicuous sign of the new prosperity—and the greatest single force behind it—is the increasing automobilization of Italy. As in the United States after World War I and in Germany after World War II, the mass marketing of autos has created new factories, jobs and paychecks in Italy by generating demand for steel, rubber, glass, brass and gas. There was only one car for every 350 Italians before World War II; now there is one for seven—compared with one for five in West Germany and one for two in the United States. Every Friday four million city dwellers pack baggage and *bambini* into their cars and, with horns shrieking and clutches crunching, take off for the country to enjoy what they call *Il Weekend*. The automobile gives them a new sense of freedom. In all, eight million cars jam the country's plazas, its poplar-lined roads and its new highways, which are already so crowded that trucks may soon be banned at peak traffic hours.

The auto-borne prosperity leads to economic and social mobility as well as to physical mobility. Sicilians and Calabrians who used to dream of emigrating to America can now find jobs in their own country. Last year 300,000 of them permanently left their farms for the northern manufacturing cities like Milan and Turin, where many work in Fiat's plants.

Propelling Prosperity

There remain shocking gaps in Italy's prosperity. Unemployment among the country's 20-million-member labor force hovers at 3.4 per cent, which is high by Western European standards. It would be higher still, but 1.5 million Italians have temporarily migrated in order to work in other European countries (one major employer: Germany's Volkswagen). In southern Italy, where many of the 18 million inhabitants live in poverty and illiteracy, per capita income is only $637. "Africa begins at Naples," goes an Italian saying about the South's leading city. Naples lives on memories, and some think that the last good one was the invasion of the fun-loving, free-spending GI's in 1944. Tens of thousands of destitute Neapolitans still exist in wretched *bassi*— basement apartments divided into "rooms" by blankets hung from lines that have been strung from wall to wall.

Now, many depressed areas are being revitalized. In Taranto, an ancient Spartan port inside the heel of the Italian boot, the government runs a model industrialization program. It has increased the city's per capita income in the past dozen years from 62 per cent of the national average to 96 per cent. The city has a Shell refinery, the major Finsider steel plant, a cement company and satellite industries, and its workers live in modern apartment blocks.

Another example of the propelling force of prosperity is the old Adriatic fishing village of Marzocca. Fifteen years ago, the sole signs of the twentieth century in Marzocca were a lone telephone and electricity in the evening. Its popula-

tion was 300—barefoot, black-hooded women, and fishermen
bound to wind and sail. But Italy's general economic strength
has created a thriving domestic tourist business, and vaca-
tioners have transformed the place. Its population has grown
to 3,000; more than a few inhabitants have changed from
bricklayers to contractors, and they have built hotels, restaurants and summer houses along fourteen miles of beach front.
Those who still fish take their catch in motorboats and send
it to market in refrigerated trucks.

Admittedly, the new affluence has turned Italy into something of a tourist's paradise lost. Leisurely lunches and long
siestas are disappearing because many Italians are too busy;
sun-baked piazzas have become parking lots. Incensed at the
din around centuries-old monuments, Roman officials have
banned cars from many historic areas. More basically, Italians
complain about the problems associated with rapid industrialization—snarled traffic, polluted air and a shortage of
services. . . .

Italians are discovering that change brings pain along
with progress. As in Japan and other recently industrialized
countries, old values are being discarded but new ones are
slow in coming. Affluence makes for mobility; mobility makes
for tension and conflicts. "Ours is a restless society," says
Guido Carli, head of the Bank of Italy. "There is upward
economic movement, but the institutions are not growing
and changing in the same way."

Affluence has shown Italians that they need not accept
the status quo, and they are demanding basic social and political changes. . . . As workers protested higher living costs
with a violent one-day general strike [in December 1968],
Italy's twenty-sixth government since 1945 resigned. . . . In
Rome, judges and lawyers staged an angry demonstration
outside the Palace of Justice to protest archaic penal codes
and an overloaded court system: too many cases for too few
judges.

Problems and Protest

Some of Italy's problems are the pains of growth. Students rightly, and riotously, protest in the streets against crammed classrooms and inadequately prepared professors. The universities were adequate when only a small upperclass elite could afford a higher education, but nearly 500,000 young Italians are now enrolled and overcrowding is becoming explosive. Many priests oppose their bishops on the issue of contraception, partly because the newly urbanized faithful can scarcely afford the large families that were an asset on the farm. As more and more women take jobs, they increasingly demand equal rights, including repeal of the old law that prescribes prison for adulterous women but not men.

Il Boom itself is a target of protest, both because it is there and because there is not more of it. Italian novelist Alberto Moravia echoes U.S. economist John Kenneth Galbraith when he complains about the affluent society: "The priority given here to goods compared with that given to social and cultural needs shows the degree of our corruption. Italian industry thinks only of the expansion of consumption. And it is not with culture, but with money, that one buys." Many of the critics, particularly the protesting student extremists, take their prosperity for granted and never knew the general privation of times past.

STRUGGLE FOR POST-FRANCO LEADERSHIP [5]

In a speech announcing his country's new constitution late in 1966, Generalissimo Francisco Franco put the case for retaining Francoism in Spain this way: "Every nation is surrounded by its own particular demons, and those of Spain are: an anarchistic spirit, a penchant for negative criticism, the disunity of men, extremism, and mutual enmity." The alternatives for Spain are clear. But with a history of demons

[5] From *Atlantic* Report by Loren Jenkins, journalist. *Atlantic*. 221:12+. Je. '68. Copyright © 1968, by The Atlantic Monthly Company, Boston, Mass. Reprinted with permission.

rampant, it is impossible to know which course Spain will follow after Franco. . . .

There is today an intense struggle for power developing, not only among Franco's opponents but among many of the diverse groups that have provided the foundation for his monolithic rule. The struggle is not a conventional clash between liberals and conservatives, but an eclectic stew of pressure groups and amorphous political "groupings." The contents include neo-Fascist Falangists and Communist workers; monarchists of various colors and anarchists; liberal democrats and socialists; old-line Francoist military men and the young technocrats who are gradually superseding them in the government. Each group is bent on molding the post-Franco era to its own conception of the future Spain.

There are three central conceptions: that of the old guard, which wants to preserve the present system, and its position in it, with as little alteration as possible; that of the reformers, who want to democratize the nation along Western European lines; and that of the monarchists, who stand between the two. The monarchists tend now toward one side, now the other, hoping to restore a king but unable to agree on what manner of society he should govern.

The tempo of the contest has hastened in recent years as an aging Franco has withdrawn from the public eye, except for ceremonial appearances and an occasional stiff televised address to the nation. The initial easing of Franco's dictatorship occurred in the first half of the decade, though it has since become apparent that meaningful reform was largely in the imaginations of foreign observers. Pressure for liberalization came in fact from pragmatists within the regime who were more interested in moving Spain into the Common Market than in adhering to an obsolete ideology.

Pragmatists or liberals, their most important reform came in 1966, and it was basic by Western republican standards: a new press law, which relaxed but did not abolish Franco's censorship. It brought a cautious political debate in the newspapers, and expectations of more radical change.

Those expectations were most apparent among the splinter
groups of former Franco supporters who became disaffected
by the political immobilism of the regime, and in the in-
effectual "opposition" which has futilely contested the Caudillo's [Franco's] rule over the years. For the first time since
the Civil War, newspapers began to run editorials about the
need to modify the institutions of government. Opposition
attacks on the regime were beefed up, and workers and students openly challenged the government to permit free
unions and democratize the nation.

Thaw

Throughout 1966 rumor of a thaw in the Spanish autocracy persisted, sustained by the fact that the Cabinet was
debating a new constitution: the Organic Law of State. This
document was supposed to create political guidelines for the
future of Spain, and to establish an institutional framework
for Franco's succession. The constitution was eagerly awaited
throughout the country as an indicator of just how far Franco
was willing to go.

Franco's announcement of the constitution in the Spanish parliament, the Cortes, at the end of 1966 was a letdown.
The key issues—labor reform, religious liberty, structural
modification of the National Movement (the only legal political organization), and the question of popular election
of some deputies to the previously appointive Cortes—were
all ambiguously stated, pending clearer statements in later
constitutional amendments. But the new constitution did
streamline the government: a premier was to be named to
take over some of the workaday labors of the government
from the chief of state (Franco). . . . The problem of succession machinery was acknowledged too by a clause em-
powering the Council of the Realm, previously an honorific
body with no real powers, to select a new chief of state,
either king or regent, if Franco should fail to do so before
retiring from the political scene. The Cortes would then
approve him.

But the liberals' hopes were too high. Today . . . it is apparent that the regime's intentions toward democracy and reform were merely flirtatious. . . . Franco's domination of Spanish politics remains unchallenged.

The key amendments clarifying Franco's general statement of the constitution emerged from the Cabinet for approval in the do-as-you're-told Cortes; they were as liberal as a suit of armor. The long-awaited religious-liberty reform was watered down and has been condemned by Protestants because of provisions to force all non-Catholic churches to register their members with the Ministry of Justice. The bill to redefine the Falange-dominated National Movement elevated the Movement's own national directorate to a form of upper house charged with arbitrating the nation's politics. Nothing was done to ease the Falange's hold over Spanish politics. When the ground rules were laid down for the popular election of one fifth of the Cortes, the game was carefully fixed in favor of National Movement candidates. . . .

Breath of Freedom

For those who still had any doubts, Franco reiterated that so long as he lived political parties would not be allowed. And the breath-of-freedom press law was decorated with a revision of the penal code to make journalists liable to six-years' imprisonment for writing "false or dangerous" information. The promised labor reform has yet to materialize. . . .

[In 1967] the ailing vice president of Spain, Captain General Agustín Muñoz Grandes, a moderate antimonarchist who once was thought certain to succeed Franco, was quietly retired. . . . He was succeeded by Admiral Luis Carrero Blanco, a Cabinet secretary, no liberal, one of Franco's most trusted background advisers since the Civil War. . . .

This swing to the right was accompanied by a campaign to silence the discord and dissent which urged the liberals on. Cries of "Democracy yes, Franco no" . . . were heard in worker districts and universities; they terrified the regime stalwarts, who equate all such statements with the chaos of the old republic. The government's reaction was swift. Meetings of anti-Franco workers were dispelled and their leaders rounded up, intellectuals and journalists were tried or fined for breaking the bounds of legitimate expression, and university activists were arrested and harassed.

Reaction lashed out just as forces for change in Spain were emerging. Franco's brief fling with liberalization did not, of course, create these new forces, as reactionaries have charged in urging Franco to curb them. But the fling did give them a season in which to flower.

The most visible—and until recently the most effective—of the new groups was that of the young technocrats in the regime who fired Spain's American-primed economic boom in the late 1950s and early 1960s. The group includes the dynamic Minister of Industry Gregorio López Bravo, Economic Planning Minister Laureano López Rodó, and Minister of Commerce Faustino García-Moncó. All three are members of the Opus Dei, the apostolic Catholic lay order which is trying to maneuver itself into a dominant position in any future government.

Hangover Quarantine

These men have found their readiest support among similarly nonideological, market-hungry industrialists eager to do business with Europe. Their political fortunes have naturally risen and fallen with the state of the economy, and as the economy flourished in the early 1960s under their tutelage and because of an unprecedented tourist boom, their stock with Franco soared. Madrid's foreign policy has really consisted of a campaign to break down the West's hangover quarantine against Hitler's passive ally Franco, and to win acceptance of Spain as an equal partner among its European neighbors. So the technocrats have attempted subtly to maneuver the regime into a position where it might qualify for the democratic criteria of the Treaty of Rome. In the early part of the decade, Spain began seeking admission to the Common Market. Madrid is now negotiating with Brussels for an associate membership which, it is hoped, would lead to full EEC membership within six years. But EEC members like Belgium and Holland do not forget Franco's alliances with Hitler and Mussolini, or overlook his commitment to authoritarianism. Because of this, the technocrats, backed by liberals outside the government, succeeded in forcing what reforms they could before the regime once more stiffened. Recent economic setbacks, however, have cut into the clout of the Opus Dei technocrats.

Black, White, and Blue

A more formidable reform bloc has sprung up in the Catholic Church, traditionally one of the foundations of Franco's power. The Ecumenical Council forced a split in Franco's church support by drawing many of the younger and more active priests away from the conservative church hierarchy. The latter, under Spain's 1953 Concordat with the Vatican, is virtually appointed by Franco. The bishops, whose mean age is sixty-eight, are fighting for control over the "new wave" priests. The latter in turn are shocked by a drop in church attendance, which they attribute to the church's embrace of the regime. Influenced by post-Pius Vatican liberalism, a whole generation of Spanish priests are beginning to speak out against the social and economic conservatism of the regime and actively to support their parishioners. In every recent workers' demonstration clerical collars have been there in black and white complement to blue-collar protest.

The toughest challenges to the regime, however, have come from worker and student groups. Labor discontent has kept pace with a flight of a dangerous inflation that the government appears unable to constrain. While Spain's economy has grown at the rate of 8 per cent annually, lifting its per capita income to almost $700 per annum in 1967, consumer demand has forced up the cost of living in the past three years by 30 per cent. . . . [In 1967] prices were hiked on everything from bread to public transportation. Despite the government's September increase in the minimum wage to 96 pesetas ($1.37) a day, salaries have failed to keep pace with the cost of living. After the recent devaluation to bring the peseta into line with the pound, the government launched an austerity drive, freezing wages and prices and cutting down on government spending in an effort to bring the economy back into balance. But austerity has only kindled labor unrest by cutting back long-sought wage increases (many of which were long ago negotiated), and the situation was aggravated by the threat of mass layoffs. U.S. plans to cut overseas investment and curb tourism are hardly a boon to Spain. But though strained by inflation and austerity, Spain's economy is basically sound and full of potential for growth. Last year [1967] brought more than seventeen million tourists, spreading ideas along with $1 billion of foreign exchange.

The government-controlled *sindicatos* (compulsory unions), which ought to serve as the vehicle through which labor could push for a better economic deal, have been more interested in neutralizing wildcat labor pressures on the economy than in challenging the status quo. The result has been a spin-out from the *sindicatos* to the new and powerful "workers commission" movement.

Catholics, Socialists, Communists, and Basque separatists have all had their own clandestine labor organizations in the past, but there was no serious opposition labor movement until the workers commissions began to evolve in 1964. The informal commissions follow the tradition of the anarcho-syndicalist movement of the early part of the century. They eschew any formal political ties, and demand that members enter as individuals and not as members of political factions. The commissions sought to weld a true labor movement around the basic economic issues facing the working classes: inflation, lagging wages, and the need for a democratic reform of the nation's labor laws. By 1967 they had become the most powerful opposition force in the nation, and, despite stiff government repression, staged three national demonstrations to demand labor reforms.

Siege on Campus

Opposition to the government is loud on campuses, but because of the transience of university populations it is ephemeral. Militant students have succeeded in Madrid, Barcelona, and Santiago de Compostela, and to a lesser extent in Seville, Bilbao, and Valencia, in doing for academia what the workers are seeking to do for industry: to supplant static, state-dominated unions with an independent democratic organization. Since the first democratic student union was installed at the University of Barcelona in 1966, over police and academic opposition, the movement has all but drowned the official Professional Students Association. . . . In its place has risen the University Students Democratic Union (SDEU). With success the SDEU has turned from initial organizational battles to more frankly political concerns such as anti-Vietnam War rallies, and skirmishes with police over attempts to hold protest marches against "the general repressive policies of the regime." At Madrid University the demonstrations are invariably broken up by the tough riot police who hover almost constantly on the edges of the campus in jeeps and trucks, supported by water cannon, mounted policemen, and German shepherds. . . .

Tendencies

Challenge to the regime has also come from the nation's meager formal opposition, which, with the exception of the small and tightly disciplined Communists, doesn't really consist of political parties. Middle-class intellectual salons are grouped around such liberal luminaries as Social Democrat José Maria Gil Robles, the former Republican minister. These groups are fractured into dozens of tendencies which, lacking unity and organization, have very little influence. Though some of the leaders and members are deeply sincere in their dislike of the regime, the opposition is not taken seriously because of its propensity for talk rather than action. Except for the Communists and regional Basque nationalists, the old parties in exile, the Anarchists and Socialists, play no role in today's Spain. They have no followers inside the nation, where completely new alignments have arisen, and because of their prolonged exile they have little grasp of what is going on in their homeland.

Behind Spain's new politics are the generations for whom the Civil War is nothing more than history—terrible history but nevertheless not a part of their experience. These generations, however politically minded, do support a relaxation of Franco's autocracy. Technicians, doctors, lawyers, businessmen, and teachers, they want a freer society. They have been nurtured on the economic boom of the past decade which has brought them cars (the ubiquitous little Spanish-built SEAT) and seaside holidays; they pay little attention to the regime's obsession with the horrors of the past. They feel entitled to the economic freedom that other Europeans have, and a form of democracy seems to them the only mechanism that will bring it.

Franco's position remains unchallenged. Though he has never been loved, he is respected, even among many who oppose his rule. Only the Communists and the impotent or exiled extremists talk today of toppling him. His support among the military, the affluent, and the church remains strong despite the young dissidents.

The issue in Spain is therefore not to change Franco, but to mold the post-Franco era. As the Caudillo envisions it, the future is to be much like the past. Parties will not be allowed, and all debate will be contained within the National Movement. The country will be run as in the past by a tight group of loyal Francoist ministers committed to keeping the faith, with a chief of state at the summit of the authoritarian pyramid.

After Franco

The question remains, Who will succeed Franco? Since 1947, Spain has been officially a monarchy without a king.

Candidates for the post abound, but the most serious are
Don Juan de Borbón y Battenberg, the exiled pretender
whose father, Alfonso XIII, was Spain's last king, and Don
Juan's thirty-year-old son, Prince Juan Carlos. Don Juan is
alienated from the regime because he is suspected of favoring
a constitutional monarchy. Prince Juan Carlos, who for a
long time was considered Franco's preference by virtue of
his more ambiguous political formation, has said that he will
never oppose his father. [However, he was invested as the
future monarch in July 1969.—Ed.] Monarchists support Don
Juan, while senior members of the administration have supported Prince Juan Carlos, who has been educated under
Franco's tutelage and now lives just down the road from his
mentor's Pardo palace. But the prince is considered by many
to be devoid of the dynamism and intelligence that would be
needed to rule Spain. The less than inspiring role played
by his brother-in-law King Constantine in Greece has also
given rise to doubts about the wisdom of placing a young
and inexperienced king on the throne.

The other possibility for Franco's succession is the ap-
pointment of a regent. Vice President Carrero Blanco and
the tough Minister of Interior, General Camilo Alonso Vega,
commander of the paramilitary police, are considered likely
candidates for the regency should the antimonarchists in the
Cabinet and the Council of the Realm win out.

In either case the quest for Francoism after Franco would
persist. If a military regency should in fact be established
it could only maintain itself through the loyalty of the army,
or of the powerful national police. The church and the affluent—those other foundations of Francoism—would probably fall away. Most observers feel a regency would give way
to military nationalism and a form of Iberian Nasserism.

The Great Unknown

The army, of course, will be the key element in any
post-Franco situation. Its sentiments, however, are the great
unknown in Spanish politics. There are powerful Francoist

elements, though they, like Franco, are aging. There is also a strong monarchist strain in the military establishment, but it too is split between Don Juan and his son. The young officer corps, and especially the colonels, are unknowns, and it is they who will ultimately be the arbiters of any changes in the present system.

A third possibility is the democratization advocated by the forces of the new Spain, but since the apparent checkmate of reform within the regime, it is unclear how this move would evolve if it could.

Quiet contacts have recently been taking place among powerful elements of the establishment, both within and outside the government, to discuss the possibilities of setting up an alternative to Francoism. Administrators, military men, industrialists, and technocrats are actually exchanging views with certain key members of the intellectual opposition and the workers commissions. Although these contacts are embryonic, they could become a united liberal force, powerful enough to impose itself on the regime, including the military. In such a case, a parliamentary democracy might be in the offing, perhaps after a quiet post-Franco palace coup.

IV. EUROPE LOOKS EAST—AND WEST

EDITOR'S INTRODUCTION

The political map of Europe still reflects the outcome of World War II. Germany is divided into two parts—one allied to the West and the other allied to the East. The city of Berlin, located in East Germany, is itself divided into U.S., Soviet, British, and French zones. The iron curtain which once existed between Western Europe and the Communist countries of Eastern Europe has been drawn aside to some extent, but contact between the two halves of Europe is far from normal.

In this context, the North Atlantic Treaty Organization has had to adjust its policies and plans to fit the changing diplomatic climate. In the 1960s, many Western statesmen spoke of détente between the two halves of Europe. They favored a gradual reduction of forces by both NATO and its eastern counterpart, the Warsaw Pact. After the Soviet intervention in Czechoslovakia in 1968, serious thought had to be given as to whether or not the cold war was on again.

This section examines East-West relations in a broad political and economic context. The first article, written by Harlan Cleveland, the United States Representative on the North Atlantic Council, spells out the reaction and response of the Western allies to the Soviet action in Czechoslovakia. Although it might have appeared that the intervention meant the end of any policy of détente, Mr. Cleveland points out that this is too hasty a conclusion. The intervention, he stresses, represented a desperate attempt to preserve the unity of the Communist bloc of nations and was not aimed at the West at all.

The second article also explores the impact and implications of the Soviet action. Recalling the historical background of Eastern Europe and the current state of affairs in the individual countries, the article examines policy alternatives open to the United States and the West.

The next article, by a former United States Ambassador to West Germany, reaffirms the need for continued close ties between the United States and Europe. But he says that the nature of the relationship needs reformulation. The existing economic and political ties between the two provide the basis for an evolving sense of common purpose which could result in true partnership.

The following two pieces review West German relations with Eastern Europe. The first article concentrates on German-Polish questions, and the second looks at West Germany in relation to all of Eastern Europe and to the Soviet Union.

The concluding article points out that if we want to talk of the future of Europe, it will be necessary to understand it in its historical context and in terms of what it has contributed to the development of civilization. The author notes that unity has never been part of the European experience. This historical perspective adds an extra dimension to an understanding of Europe today and even suggests a formula for policies of the future.

NATO AFTER THE INVASION [1]

It was the third week in August 1968 and the North Atlantic allies were relaxing on their beaches, in their mountains and in their chancelleries too. There was plenty to relax about, for 1968 had started as a big year for détente in Europe. The East-West exchange in political leaders was at an all-time high; a Western leader who had not recently been in Poland or Rumania was hardly alive politically unless he was home preparing to receive his opposite number from Hungary or Bulgaria. The Mayor of Moscow was in The Hague;

[1] From article by Harlan Cleveland, U.S. permanent representative on the North Atlantic Council. *Foreign Affairs.* 47:251-65. Ja. '69. Reprinted by special permission from *Foreign Affairs*, January 1969. Copyright by the Council on Foreign Relations, Inc., New York.

the Red Army Choir was about to entertain in the concert halls of England; the University of Minnesota Band was practicing for its trip to the Soviet Union. The John F. Kennedy Airport was braced for the second ceremonial Aeroflot flight, part of the new nonstop service between Moscow and New York. In Moscow, carpenters were hammering together a big Italian trade fair. And in Washington, the White House was working hard on the possibility of talks with the Soviet Union about strategic nuclear missile and antimissile systems.

The atmospheric improvement in East-West relations was matched by a growing clarity in the West that making peace with the Russians would require a judicious mix of collective desire and collective defense. In May 1968 the NATO Defense Ministers, meeting in Brussels,

reaffirmed the need for the Alliance to maintain an effective military capability and to assure a balance of forces between NATO and the Warsaw Pact in Europe and elsewhere. . . . Ministers endorsed the proposition that the overall military capability of NATO should not be reduced except as part of a pattern of mutual force reductions balanced in scope and timing.

Then in June [1968] at a Reykjavik [Iceland] meeting, NATO's Foreign Ministers signed a Declaration which, in effect, invited the Soviets and their Warsaw Pact allies to negotiate about mutual and balanced force reductions in Europe—while repeating their determination to maintain NATO's defensive capability. NATO was so credibly anxious to move beyond static peacekeeping to dynamic peacemaking that in the Norwegian Storting an antimilitaristic left could without embarrassment join a Conservative government in passing a pro-NATO measure by a vote of 144 to 6. The Western democracies, their competitive spirit aroused, had dipped their toes in "coexistence" and found they could live with it. Defense and détente had been glued together for the difficult period of "peaceful engagement" assumed to be just around the corner.

Then the Warsaw Five [the Soviet Union, East Germany, Poland, Hungary, and Bulgaria] moved into Czechoslovakia, and showed that the Soviet leaders are no longer so sure they can live with competitive coexistence themselves.

Very few Europeans or Americans can honestly say they correctly predicted this enormous event. Most of them were holding in their heads two propositions we now perceive as contradictory: first, that the Czechoslovak liberalization program would be fatal to the Communist system; second, that the Soviets would inveigh but not invade.

The experts and intelligence analysts soon testified that the Russian move was perfectly rational and indeed inevitable from the Soviet point of view. Being professionals, most of them could even point to passages in their own writings which "did not exclude" an invasion. But the truth is that few experts really thought of invasion as a rational move before the event; Budapest 1956 was regarded as one of a kind. Perhaps Western experts should be excused for underrating the will of the Soviets to use force in Czechoslovakia; so did Rumania's Ceaucescu and Tito—not to mention Alexander Dubcek.

Why did the Russians do it? Because they decided that their hold on the Warsaw Pact countries had first priority—ahead of East-West relations in Europe, ahead of Soviet-American relations, even ahead of Russian leadership in the world Communist movement.

"The defense of socialism in Czechoslovakia is not only the internal affair of the people of that country," said *Pravda* on August 22. "Can a country wrested from the Socialist community really safeguard its genuine sovereignty?" asked *Izvestia* on August 24. The Warsaw Pact nations "have the right of self-defense," Poland's Gomulka argued on September 8, "when the enemy mines our own house, the community of Socialist states, with dynamite." "Marxism is irreconcilable with nationalism no matter how 'just,' 'clean,' fine or civilized the latter may be," *Soviet Russia* declared on September 11. "Neutrality for the Socialist countries means alienation from the Socialist camp," said *Pravda Ukrainy* on September 14.

Sovereignty has thus been collectivized—at least for the purpose of justifying, ex post facto, the invasion and occupation of Czechoslovakia. It took until September 26 for the Soviets to work out a full-blown intellectual defense of their August 20 action, but when it appeared in *Pravda* it was nothing if not perfectly clear. The particular must give way to the "general" (read Soviet) interest; "the sovereignty of each Socialist country cannot be opposed to the interests of the world of socialism." Sovereignty, as preached and practiced by unidentified anti-Socialist elements in Czechoslovakia, would have enabled NATO troops to "come up to the Soviet border, while the community of European Socialist states would have been split." In such conditions "law and legal norms are subordinated to the laws of the class struggle."

An older Soviet adage said it less bureaucratically and more frankly: "Law is like the tongue of a wagon—it goes in the direction in which it is pointed."

The forces of the Warsaw Pact began moving at 11 P.M. the evening of August 20. A couple of hours later, in Paris, London, Washington and some other capitals, Soviet Ambassadors hastened to deliver assurances that the tanks and planes were in Prague by invitation, and were not directed against the "state interests" of the United States or other Allies. At 2 A.M., August 21, Prague radio aired news of the invasion; at 2:09 the Associated Press carried its first "flash," based on the Prague broadcast. Meanwhile some of NATO's air defense radars were partially jammed—a by-product of Soviet jamming in Czechoslovakia, as it turned out. By breakfast time in Europe, the NATO "crisis-consultation" machinery was in high gear.

The first big debate inside NATO was not about long-term policy but on a disturbing tactical question: Why didn't we know the invaders were going to move before they moved?

For NATO strategists, the question is no side issue. NATO's flexible strategy rests heavily on the assumption that the West would have two kinds of warning of any move by the Warsaw Pact against NATO. We would have political warning, because a surprise attack not preceded by a build-up of political tensions seems almost inconceivable. We would have strategic warning, because we would see and sense the build-up of forces the Soviets would require to undertake a serious military operation against the NATO defense system. But it has always seemed unlikely that we could tell in advance the precise moment at which an attack by those built-up forces would be launched. So the doctrine has been: There shouldn't be any such thing as political surprise or strategic surprise, but tactical surprise is always possible.

In the first shock of seeing Russian troops just across the Bavarian border, this whole set of assumptions was called into serious question. But if anything, the events of August show that our warning doctrine stands up pretty well. We (and the Czechoslovaks) had eight months of quite visible political warning—the Soviets had been visibly distressed ever since Dubcek came into power. We had a number of weeks of strategic warning, as the Soviet forces got into position to threaten the Czech leaders with a military invasion.

As far as it went, therefore, our analysis in NATO was about right: the Soviets, we thought, were massing most of their strength in Eastern Europe on the Czech border. NATO correctly guessed that these very large military movements—the largest in Europe since the Second World War—were not aimed against NATO; they were designed either to pressure the Czechs or, if the pressure failed, to be ready for invasion. What we didn't know was whether they would invade—until they started to move, and told us they were moving. Certainly the military plan was laid long before all the negotiating and palavering. . . . But the political decision was evidently taken quite late in the game.

The Soviet military move was impressively rapid, well planned and well executed. It was of course massively overdone to meet the contingency of armed resistance: more than one third of a million men, more than twenty-five ground divisions, some airlifted from as far away as the Baltic regions, and the occupation of all the large airfields in Czechoslovakia. Yet this efficient operation was in the service of an almost childishly sloppy political scenario.

The Soviets' poor political planning, and the passive but remarkable resistance of the Czechs, made quite a drama for a few days. The first quick assumption was that once the Soviets set their mind to it, the deed was as good as done. The troops rolled in, the airfields were taken, the borders sealed; then something went wrong. If the Soviets achieved tactical military surprise, the Czechs achieved a tactical political surprise by keeping their government in being and in motion—and in communication with the outside world. Czech diplomats remained busy and at work at the UN and in foreign capitals, still in touch with a government in Prague which astonishingly was neither controlled nor swept aside by the otherwise efficient Soviet forces. The Czechoslovak radio and press networks went underground, and the world could actually witness the arrival of Soviet tanks filmed by Czech television cameramen and relayed by the Czech television network to Eurovision.

In the end, that much power was bound to prevail—for the time being—over the stubborn, resourceful and embarrassing passive resistance of the Czech leaders and people. In a quick change of plans, the Soviets "negotiated" with their prisoners and elicited what amounted to an "invitation"—retroactively, with duress, in a communiqué issued not from Prague but from Moscow. Another arm-twisting negotiation in October confirmed Prague's agreement to a Soviet garrison of indefinite duration. Just how many Soviet troops will stay is not important: whatever troops the Soviets keep in Czechoslovakia will be enough to make sure they can bring more in whenever necessary. And they will stay as long as Moscow pleases.

What does all this mean for Western security? The quick answer—too quick—is that détente is dead and the cold war is back on. Once again at a moment of doubt and disarray, the Soviets have done something to illustrate for the doubters the case for hanging together. Their takeover of Czechoslovakia in 1948 helped pass the Marshall Plan; the invasion of 1968 sidetracked the Mansfield Resolution and the Symington Amendment, which called for pulling U.S. troops out of Europe. But 1969 is not 1949 all over again.

In 1949 the Communists thought one big war was inevitable. The Soviets were just testing their first atomic bomb, and thought they were in an arms race against us; now they (and we) find the race was really against time, and we both won it in the sense of achieving a capability for assured destruction no matter who strikes first. Then (in 1949), a would-be monolithic movement, run by one dictator, was promoting and presiding over world communism; now (in 1969) a collective leadership is busy trying to hang onto a dependable socialism-in-one-region. Then the Soviet empire was expanding; now its rulers are trying by force to prevent it from coming apart.

In short, the invasion of Czechoslovakia can be read as the latest and most dramatic spasm in the nervous decomposition of the "Socialist commonwealth" and the attempt by its bosses to arrest the rot by repression. The result is a range of dangers, but also some opportunities, which are neither the cold war of our bygone fears nor the warm détente of our recent dreams.

The East-West military confrontation in Europe is certainly more acute than it was before. There are, quite simply, more Soviet troops, farther west, in a higher state of readiness than before . . . [the summer of 1968]. It is true that the large Soviet troop movements were directed against their own allies and not against ours. But there is more to intentions than current plans of action. There are many ways in which turbulence and terror inside the Warsaw Pact area could spill over onto NATO's frontiers.

The collective decision to beef up NATO's military strength, and the national decisions to invest more men and money in NATO-committed forces, were caused less by the sudden rise in Soviet military readiness than by the quantum jump in uncertainty about Soviet behavior. If the Soviet leaders could misread as badly as they did their near neighbors, the Czechs, how well are they reading us today?

The disturbing fact is that we do not really know what the Soviet leaders have in mind. They have said all too clearly that they propose to hang onto their empire no matter what. But how big is the empire they have chosen to "defend"? How far beyond the Warsaw Pact does the "Socialist commonwealth" extend? Rumania is hard-line Communist on the inside; how independent an external policy can Bucharest get away with? Is Yugoslavia a link in the "chain of Socialist states"? In whose "camp" do the Soviet leaders place Albania today—or will they tomorrow? Beyond Communist rule there are other European lands not part of the NATO defense system which we have been assuming were safe from Soviet "protection" but where new anxieties have arisen.

On the first day of the Czechoslovak crisis, a perceptive European made this relevant comment in a NATO meeting: "The Russians have said they're serious about protecting their harem, but they haven't said how big it is." Trying to limit it by preventive diplomacy, fifteen foreign ministers, meeting as the North Atlantic Council . . ., warned the Soviets that any more interventions "would create an international crisis with grave consequences."

The first reaction of the North Atlantic Alliance to the mounting Czech crisis—before the invasion—was to watch carefully but lie low. Despite the big build-up of Warsaw Pact forces around Czechoslovakia, despite their vigorous maneuvers not far from NATO's borders, the political judgment (that this threat was directly against a Pact ally, not against the NATO alliance) led to agreed Allied policy: scrupulously to avoid giving the Russians any Western excuse to move into Czechoslovakia.

This restraint was not, as restraint so often is, the paralysis of timidity. It was a conscious policy consensus in the North Atlantic Council. It did not save the Czechs, of course; nor was it intended to. But the policy "worked" in the sense of helping to make ridiculously unbelievable the pathetic attempts to pin the ideological "crimes" of the Czechoslovak leaders on "imperialists" and other dark forces of external subversion.

When the Russians struck, NATO was readier for round-the-clock crisis management than it had ever been before. For one thing, when NATO's political headquarters was moved from Paris to Brussels in October 1967, the Council decided to build into the new headquarters a modern Situation Room, complete with up-to-date visual aids and serviced by a new NATO-wide communication system. And the Council's Committee of Political Advisers, in earlier times a once-a-week mutual information society, had been converted to an everyday "watch committee" producing overnight political assessments to guide NATO's military commanders. These facilities proved their value as the Allies turned immediately to consulting together about what had happened, and what it meant for Western security.

The Council's first political decision after the invasion was to continue to lie low—to take some obvious precautions but not to imply by a noisy alert or mobilization that there was a sudden danger to the West. Nothing, it was felt, should be done to distract from the efforts to condemn the Soviet invasion in the UN Security Council.

But behind the scenes the invasion had brought into being a NATO work program of impressive and exhausting scope—a book of lessons learned from the invasion about Soviet logistics and mobility and tactics, a special inquiry into the "warning" issue, a reestimate of Soviet intentions, a complex consultation about the dampening of East-West contacts, a study on the economic implications, a revision of plans for regional arms-control proposals, and a new look at NATO's force plans in the light of the new uncertainties. The first product of the intensive daily work—"drafting by night and tearing it to pieces by day"—emerged . . . when NATO's Defense Planning Committee (a euphemism for the North Atlantic Council when it meets without France) published a declaration marking the end of the "lie-low" policy. The statement reminded a suddenly attentive world of the defense-cum-détente policy formalized by NATO ministers at their May and June meetings. Prospects for mutual force reductions having "suffered a severe setback," the NATO nations said they proposed to maintain their military capabilities, and announced a thorough assessment of NATO's forces in the light of "recent developments in Eastern Europe."

In effect, this was a pledge that there would be no reduction of forces pending comprehensive analysis and deliberate decision making by the Council. It was needed as a stopgap policy because many of the Allies were well into a process of trimming defense budgets, shaving their contributions to NATO, relaxing their readiness levels and neglecting standards for weapons and stocks. The natural urge to save money on the defense establishment had been reinforced by apparent symptoms of a growing détente.

To shift gears, from reverse to forward, is hard enough inside a single government; in an international organization the task is compounded by a factor somewhat greater than the number of its members. An international organization moves by fits and starts, and the fits are called ministerial meetings. Western Europe's first reaction to the Czech invasion was to assume that NATO would call a special meeting of Foreign and Defense ministers—[former West German] Chancellor Kiesinger even suggested a meeting at summit level—to stress Alliance solidarity and rebuild the Western defense system.

The other NATO nations began by looking to Washington for a cue. Somewhat to their surprise, Washington passed the initiative back to them: a great gathering of NATO ministers would be useful only when each government had had time to give its allies "concrete indications" of what it thought it could do to enhance its contribution to the NATO defense system. We should know the denouement before turning on the drama.

None of the other potential leaders—the Germans, the British, the Italians—quite felt able to step forward and break the multilateral game of "Après vous, Alphonse." And the smaller Allies, considering it a big crisis, thought the big countries should take the lead. Thus for a variety of reasons —all related to their internal politics—none of the members wanted to blow the opening whistle and suggest a new target for NATO after Czechoslovakia. Yet most said privately that they could do more for NATO if NATO asked for more to be done. The problem was to put together concrete national steps in the form of a "collective initiative" in which no member seemed to be out in front, and to which each member could respond. This was a job for the Council in Permanent Session. In time, with mutual prodding, there were enough "concrete indications" of added defense efforts to justify moving up to mid-November the regular December meeting of NATO ministers.

It was a foregone conclusion that the collective Western defense system would have to be strengthened. As the meetings were held, the deficiencies unveiled, the plans for improvement laid and the cost of alertness calculated, a wide consensus was soon evident on what kind of collective response NATO should make. (The question of exactly who should do exactly what, for how much, at whose expense, naturally took a little longer.) Before the end of September, NATO's fourteen active defenders had decided that what was needed was not so much *more,* as *better* forces. If the Soviets are readier, NATO had better be readier. If Soviet behavior is less predictable, then NATO needed an even more flexible "flexible response" strategy, with all that implies for mobility and trained reserves and speed of reaction in a crisis.

NATO's force goals—part of a five-year defense-planning system to accompany the "flexible response"—are a blend of military requirements and the resources likely to be available. They have a built-in "carrot factor," or incentive gap, of about 10 per cent between the feasible and the desirable.

The post-Czechoslovakia plans are, by and large, to try to meet the full force goals immediately. Every NATO ally has latterly been below NATO standards of manning, equipment and training; the Allies quickly agreed that each of them should try to meet the agreed standards. The Mobile Force that serves Allied Command Europe is to be enlarged. NATO-committed tactical air forces, which have been too largely reserved for the "least likely eventuality" of general nuclear war, are to be converted more rapidly for use in less glamorous but more relevant conventional roles—tactical bombing, close support, air defense, reconnaissance. And the much-discussed "transatlantic bargain," whereby the Europeans improve their capacity to mobilize ready reserves in a hurry and the North American members improve their capacity to provide air and ground reinforcements in a hurry, is also part of the "collective response."

Some of the new effort is being applied outside of Central Europe, which naturally got most of the attention at first because that was where Czechoslovakia happened to be. NATO was already planning, for example, to take on as an Alliance responsibility the surveillance of Soviet naval activities in the Mediterranean and to organize an "on call" NATO naval unit for special exercises and limited emergencies. New anxieties about the future of Yugoslavia and Albania stirred in NATO's Mediterranean allies an even livelier interest in organizing NATO-committed naval power so that it would be usable in something short of a general war. A NATO Command of Maritime Air Forces for the Mediterranean was officially established in November; its program will include use of some planes newly based by the United Kingdom in Malta, as well as those provided by the Italian and U.S. forces in the area.

Beefing up the NATO defense system is going to cost money, and much of the maneuvering by each Ally to get the others to speak up first was occasioned by the enormous difficulty each government perceived in reversing a budget-cutting trend already well started between 1967 and 1968.

In reporting their defense plans to NATO, the twelve participants other than the United States said last year they expected to spend upwards to $90 billion over the five-year period 1968-72. Taken together, they have been using just under 5 per cent of their gross national product for defense purposes. (We spend about 10 per cent of our GNP for defense, but that of course includes the heavy budgetary burden of the war in Vietnam; the "pure" U.S. contribution to NATO would run well under 2 per cent, even if our Atlantic Navy and all our nuclear weapons in the theatre are included.) But in 1968 our allies' spending was down to 4.5 per cent of GNP. The first essential will be to turn this Allied spending curve back up; for the Allies other than the United States, a total expenditure of $100 billion, rather than $90 billion, might be a reasonable target over the next five years.

The new pledges of men, matériel and money, announced at the November 14 ministerial meeting of NATO, were a big step in this direction. And for the first time in Alliance history, the lion's share—80 to 90 per cent of the new effort —was contributed by the Europeans.

The Soviet action in Czechoslovakia was a deep wound to the agreed Western policy of pursuing détente between East and West. During the last ten days of August every NATO country hastened to dampen contacts, postpone political visits and generally defer the building of East-West bridges. The Minnesota Band did not visit the Soviet Union, and the Red Army Choir was not heard in England. The Mayor of Moscow was shipped hurriedly out of The Hague. Ministers in half a dozen Western countries who had been preparing trips designed to bolster their personal contributions to peace, suddenly discovered urgent business at home. Diplomatic parties celebrating Polish Army Day, the Bolshevik Revolution and the like were boycotted by all but minor Western officials. The Italian fair in Moscow went on, but when in a show of business as usual the top Soviet leaders turned up as visitors, they found no Italian official of comparable rank had made the trip.

All these moves were the product of quick, instinctive agreement, made explicit in political consultations at NATO headquarters in Brussels; nobody wanted to be accused of acting chummy with the Warsaw Five in the fall of 1968. But how long should the period of mourning be? The more difficult policy choices are in the longer range.

The rationale for all this East-West bridge building, all these cultural exchanges and reciprocal political visits, has been the underlying assumption that the limits of tolerance in Moscow would permit the highly differentiated impulses in Eastern Europe toward independence, toward internal reform, toward easier and closer relations with the West to help bring about gradually, and perhaps erratically, a sea change in the climate of East-West relations. This process was seen as a prerequisite for a renewed approach to the fundamental issues which have divided Europe for more than two decades; and it is only by resolving these fundamental issues that one can begin to think seriously about a "European security system" that is any improvement over a stalemated balance of military forces.

Assumptions of this sort were fundamental to West Germany's *Ostpolitik,* to France's decision to pull out of NATO's military work, to the British interest in an East-West "code of conduct," to the beginning of "special relationships" between several pairs of states on opposite sides of the dividing line, and to the Group of Ten—an informal small-country forum of NATO countries, Warsaw Pact members and European neutrals. The sense that things were loosening up in the East was equally fundamental to [former] President [Lyndon] Johnson's bridge-building policy; in a major policy speech October 7, 1967, he pressed Congress to act on U.S.-Soviet consular relations, loosened controls on East-West trade, allowed the Export-Import Bank to guarantee commercial credits to more East European countries and spoke of easing the Polish debt burden, helping the Fiat auto plant in Russia, liberalizing travel, completing the U.S.-Soviet civil air agreement and exchanging photographs taken from weather satellites.

The Russian leaders have now made it brutally plain that the efforts of the Dubcek regime to create a "Socialist humanism" went well beyond the limits of their tolerance for change in Eastern Europe. If each step toward liberalization or closer relations with the West produces another turn of the repressive screw in the East, the NATO allies are face-to-face with an excruciating policy dilemma. Peacemaking efforts by Western leaders will run into more political criticism at home; "détente politics," which assisted many European ministers to power, will lack the thrust it had in European politics before August 20.

The new obstacles to disarmament dealings with the Communists are especially obvious. On August 20 [1968] NATO's hand was outstretched, holding a proposal to talk seriously with the Eastern allies about arms control in Europe. The desire for détente is so deep, in the domestic politics of the NATO allies, that this welcoming hand will probably not be clenched into a fist. But the staff work on "balanced and mutual force reductions," the building of models, the development of concrete proposals, are bound to be accorded a low priority within Western governments and in NATO until the Soviets give some sign that they are thinking hard about them too.

The sharpest dilemma of all presented itself when the Johnson Administration had to face the question of whether and when to talk to the Soviets about the limitation of strategic nuclear missiles and antimissile systems. Before the invasion, Canada and our European partners were unanimous in urging us to get on with strategic arms limitation talks. Immediately after the invasion, just to set a date and begin such talks with the Soviets would have been widely resented. And it was not in the U.S.—or Allied—interest to help the Soviets wipe out the stain of Czechoslovakia by conducting business as usual.

On the other hand, the case for trying to do something about the nuclear missile race, and do it soon, is simply overwhelming; subjects that even possibly bear on survival cannot long be postponed for the sake of appearances. We are at one of those historic moments when technology has made possible another great leap in history's costliest and most terrifying arms race: we have learned how to shoot at incoming missiles, and at the same time we have learned how to multiply the number of warheads in each offensive missile. If both the United States and the Soviet Union exploit to the limit the known technologies, the mutual escalation will add enormously to the cost, while if anything subtracting from the security each side would be trying to buy with the extra billions of dollars and rubles. We cannot know, from their mere agreement to talk, whether the Soviet leaders have at last concluded, or are open to persuasion, that the next phase of this arms race makes no more sense for them than it does for us. But if there is even a fractional possibility that we could get some agreement on this cosmic complex of life-and-death issues, it would be madness to pass it up.

It is too early to judge what the new Soviet doctrines, backed by Soviet forces, may do to the Western Alliance system in the long run, but it is already clear that the long run has been lengthened. Even before the invasion of Czechoslovakia, it was apparent that no NATO ally was seriously proposing to avail itself of the provision by which signatories of the North Atlantic Treaty can, after the twentieth birthday of its coming into force—that is, after August 24, 1969— give one year's notice of withdrawal from its obligations and protections. The betting was that even France, which participates in political consultation while standing aside from the NATO defense system, would stay in the Alliance in its special way. Now, at a stroke, the Warsaw Five have solved what remained of the much-debated question: After 1969, what of NATO?

The authoritative answer was provided by the foreign ministers of NATO in the communiqué issued after their moved-up annual meeting. Skirting the kind of formal commitment that would constitute an amendment to the withdrawal clause of the Treaty (and would therefore have to be ratified by legislatures), the ministers declared on November 16, 1968:

The North Atlantic Alliance will continue to stand as the indispensable guarantor of security and the essential foundation for the pursuit of European reconciliation. By its constitution the Alliance is of indefinite duration. Recent events have further demonstrated that its continued existence is more than ever necessary.

In what amounted to a concurring opinion, French Foreign Minister Michel Debré adapted some 1966 language of General de Gaulle to add that "unless events in the years to come were to bring about a radical change in East-West relations, the French government considers that the Alliance must continue as long as it appears to be necessary." And Secretary of State Dean Rusk let it be known that the U.S. intention to stick with NATO "for the foreseeable future" was bipartisan U.S. policy checked out earlier that week with [then] President-elect Nixon.

It also seems probable that this Alliance will continue, despite Czechoslovakia, to consider its task to be defense-cum-détente—the preservation of Western security as the essential basis for making peace with the East. In the midst of all the autumn talk about beefing up European defenses, the NATO allies had no difficulty at all in agreeing that "the only political goal consistent with Western values is that of secure, peaceful and mutually beneficial relations between East and West."

But peacemaking takes two or more. The prospect for getting back on the road toward détente in Europe is deeply shadowed by the very fact of the Soviet invasion, no matter what happens next in Czechoslovakia itself. The Soviet fear of man's natural instinct for freedom will for some little time force NATO to concentrate, more than its members would prefer, on the peacekeeping side of its dual personality— while its latent peacemaking function awaits better days and brighter prospects.

The Russians may have the raw power to contain with tanks and terror the growing desire of the East Europeans for the decencies of freedom and the niceties of life. But repression cannot indefinitely smother expectations in the East which are produced, not by NATO's machinations but by the yearnings of people for a more humane society— nourished, to be sure, by the lively example of more liberal life in the West. A cartoon in a European newspaper last fall managed to say it all in a single caption. It showed a group of students and workers standing on a street corner, discussing politics with animation. In the background, two Russian commissars are wringing their hands, and one of them is saying to the other: "The trouble with all these people's democratic republics is that they seem to be producing democratic republican people."

CZECHOSLOVAKIA, RUSSIA AND EASTERN EUROPE [2]

By the dawn's early light, the Red Army tanks rumbled into Prague. Few observers had denied that it could happen. But when it did happen—when Czechoslovakia awoke on Wednesday, August 21, 1968, to a Soviet-led invasion—the world was aghast. A loyal and peaceful partner of the Soviet Union, a nation united in support of its Communist leaders, was being overrun by five of its Communist allies. . . . Cruel memories were evoked: Nazi tanks crushing the Czechoslovaks in 1939; Soviet tanks crushing the East Germans in 1953, the Hungarians in 1956. . . .

Could the Czechoslovaks hope to retain any of the liberal reforms introduced during the preceding seven and a half

[2] From *Great Decisions 1969*. (Fact Sheet no 1) Foreign Policy Association. 345 E. 46th St. New York 10017. '69. p 1-12. Copyright 1969 by the Foreign Policy Association, Inc. Reprinted by permission.

months by Communist party secretary Alexander Dubcek and his colleagues? Or would the Dubcek regime's experiment in "democratic socialism" be stamped out by the Stalinist brand of despotism?

Could other Communist nations of Eastern Europe hope to continue their recent evolution toward greater autonomy within the Soviet sphere? Or had the doctrine of "different roads to socialism" been exposed as a fraud—a principle to which the Russians pay lip service, a practice which they are swift to punish when they feel their own interests endangered?

Could the rest of the world hope that the Soviet Union, with its awesome capacity for nuclear destruction, was being guided by rational and responsible men? Or did the invasion of Czechoslovakia signify a dangerously irresponsible leadership in Moscow, subject to unpredictable fits of militarism?

Most crucial of all to American and other Western policy makers, what hopes now remained for East-West coexistence —the mutual renunciation of force and search for accommodation by the two competing systems? [See "NATO After the Invasion," in this section, above.]

Confrontation, Coexistence, Cooperation

As the West sees it, the cold-war confrontation in Europe will finally end only (a) when East and West Germans can be reunited through free all-German elections, and (b) when the peoples of Eastern Europe can run their own affairs free from dictation by Moscow.

This second goal appeared hopeless as long as Eastern Europe's Communist rulers behaved as Moscow's puppets. But after 1956 a number of Soviet-bloc regimes set forth on the "different roads to socialism" designated by former Soviet Premier Nikita Khrushchev. The solid Communist bloc constructed by Stalin after World War II visibly cracked. A revival of nationalism, a relaxation of controls and a partial reconciliation of the people with their one-party governments were the order of the day in parts of Eastern Europe.

Western statesmen, from Washington to Bonn, found cause for optimism in this new, "national Communist" look. Conceivably, it might evolve into some form of popular self-determination for Eastern Europeans, if only within a liberalized Communist structure. Hopefully, it could gradually lead Eastern and Western Europeans beyond peaceful co-existence to productive cooperation.

To this end, the United States and most of its allies have in recent years pursued a policy of détente (relaxation of coldwar tensions) and "building bridges" (commercial and cultural exchanges) with the U.S.S.R. and several of its allies. . . .

Where the East Begins

In current usage, the term "Eastern Europe" usually denotes six Soviet-bloc nations: Bulgaria, Czechoslovakia, the German Democratic Republic (GDR, or East Germany), Hungary, Poland and Rumania. Geographically and even politically, the term is anything but accurate.

From the Elbe river, dividing the two Germanies, to the mouth of the Danube on Rumania's Black Sea coast, it embraces much of Central as well as Eastern Europe. It excludes the Soviet Union itself, which is "European" as far east as the Ural mountains, Albania (see below) and also Yugoslavia, which broke clear of the bloc over twenty years ago; all three are often treated independently in the literature on Communist Europe.

For convenience, the European regimes formally allied to the Soviet Union are classified Eastern. They are linked both militarily and economically in: (1) The Warsaw Pact, a military alliance controlled by Moscow and formed in response to NATO; (2) The Council for Mutual Economic Assistance (Comecon), also dominated by Moscow and organized to coordinate economic activity among the member nations.

A seventh member of the bloc, Albania, formally withdrew from the Warsaw Pact . . . September [1968]. (Since the early 1960s, when Albanian party chief Enver Hoxha switched allegiance from Moscow to Peking, his country had belonged to the alliance in name only.) The remaining six members comprise nearly 103 million people and cover an area smaller than Texas and New Mexico combined. Together they rank as the world's fourth industrial complex (after the United States, U.S.S.R. and Western Europe), thanks to the highly developed industry of two bloc nations, East Germany and Czechoslovakia. In 1967 their total foreign trade of $26 billion surpassed all of Latin America's, although more than half of that trade was within the Comecon area.

Militarily, the six countries' regular armed forces total over a million men—equivalent to the combined forces of France, West Germany and the Netherlands. But they lean on their super-power ally for strategic defense and command decisions. The Warsaw Pact's entire nuclear arsenal is manufactured and maintained in the U.S.S.R. Its planning staff has always been headquartered in Moscow and headed by a Soviet marshal. Until last summer's invasion of Czechoslovakia, about 320,000 Soviet troops (26 divisions including support troops) were stationed in the bloc: 20 divisions in East Germany, 4 in Hungary, 2 in Poland.

Divide and Rule

Subjugation by powerful neighbors is nothing new for the peoples of Eastern Europe. For centuries the region was regarded as Europe's "borderland" or "backyard," ripe for imperial conquest and partition.

Not one of today's bloc countries, for example, appears on the map for the year 1795. Their inhabitants were divided up among the ruling Hapsburgs of Austria, the Hohenzollerns of Prussia, the Romanovs of Russia and the Ottoman sultans of Turkey. At other moments in history the map is dotted with independent kingdoms (Poland, Bohemia, Hungary) and with mythical-sounding provinces (Moldavia, Transylvania, Ruthenia). The frontiers were always shifting, the territories swelling or shrinking, as the peoples of the East clashed with their foreign conquerors and among themselves.

The fierce rivalry among the East's ethnic and religious factions inhibited the kind of nationalism that flourished in the West after the Renaissance. Today, even if we exclude the melting pot of Yugoslavia, the region exhibits tremendous diversity for its size. It encompasses four distinct Slav branches (Poles, Czechs, Slovaks, Bulgars); Germans; the Magyars of Hungary; the Latins of Rumania; as well as Ukrainians, Belorussians, Jews, gypsies and smaller ethnic minorities.

Roman Catholicism predominates in Poland, Czechoslovakia and Hungary; Eastern Orthodoxy, in Rumania and Bulgaria; Protestantism, in East Germany. Most states have sizable religious minorities.

A Vicious Circle

By 1920 this region was constituted more or less along its present national lines. World War I had liberated the subjects of the Hapsburg and Ottoman empires to create new, independent states. But many of the states had dissatisfied minorities and weak or unpopular governments. With gloomy foresight the Hungarian prime minister, Count Stephen Bethlen, observed in 1926 that ". . . fate has provided us with a breathing spell for the beginning of a new life. But how long is this state of affairs going to persist? There can be no doubt at all . . . that the great Russian nation is going to become a factor in world politics sooner or later, and that the great German nation will also recuperate from its defeat."

The great German nation had first crack. Between 1938 and 1944, Hitler's Third Reich annexed the Czechs, annihilated six million Poles and devastated their country, and dominated the Slovaks, Hungarians, Rumanians and Bulgarians through local pro-Fascist regimes.

When the Nazis were finally beaten back from Eastern Europe by the Red Army, the region lay helpless, a ready prey for Stalin. One by one, its components fell to the Communists—through military conquest, through diplomatic deals, through coups d'état or subversive coalition governments.

By late 1948 the Communist bloc (minus maverick Yugoslavia) was complete. On the map, except for East Germany and a few lesser territorial changes, it resembled the prewar map of sovereign Eastern European nations. But politically its people had reverted to a much older past. Once again, through their local puppet rulers, they were the hapless subjects of an alien empire. . . .

Three Aspects of Autonomy

National communism in Eastern Europe has exhibited three distinct aspects:

(1) *Economic decentralization.* The Stalinist system of rigid central control gives way to a more flexible "market socialism." Details vary from country to country, but the major reform features are consistent:

Profit, rather than sheer output, is a prime measure of industrial success. To show profits, state-owned factories are expected to supply the demands of the market with the same competitive efficiency as capitalist enterprises.

To this end, the managers of individual factories receive fewer directives from the state's central planners. Instead, they exercise independent judgment in many day-to-day operations: fixing product lines, reinvesting profits, choosing suppliers and sales outlets, setting wages, bonuses and other personnel incentives and, in some cases, prices. At the same time, more of the state's investment budget is allotted to light industry to satisfy consumer wants.

In agriculture, reform usually entails higher wages for employees of state collective farms and higher prices for their produce. Also, farmers may be permitted larger amounts of land for private plots—the acreage they can cultivate privately apart from their regular jobs on collective farms.

Private enterprise also expands in the personal-service sector—restaurants, dressmaking, barbershops, shoe repair—where small, family-owned and -operated businesses are tolerated.

(2) *Independent international behavior.* The Eastern European nations may forge new commercial, cultural and even diplomatic links beyond the bloc with Western or non-aligned nations without Moscow's approval. It has been said that the Iron Curtain came to resemble an iron sieve. But the bloc countries are still firmly welded by bilateral treaties —trade, security, friendship and cooperation—within the Warsaw Pact and Comecon structure.

(3) *Political liberalization.* Communist totalitarianism thaws out—within carefully prescribed channels. Citizens may be free to criticize the regime's bureaucratic shortcomings; to produce nonconformist plays and other cultural works; to enjoy access to Western radio, publications and visitors, and even to travel in the West themselves; to emulate the most successful technical and cultural achievements of non-Communist societies.

No New Titos

Bordering on three bloc countries is Europe's supreme showcase of national communism: Yugoslavia. The Balkan maverick was angrily banished from the Stalinist herd in 1948. Later on, President Josip Broz Tito repaired his rift with the Kremlin without returning to its fold. He pursues a doggedly independent course—allied to no one, agreeable to trade and aid from anyone, ambitious for a major diplomatic role in the councils of the world's nonaligned nations (Egypt, India, Pakistan, Indonesia, etc.).

Tito's poor, polytechnic nation is beset by chronic economic and social problems. Yet he has so far decentralized and democratized the Marxist system as to make Yugoslavia a worker's paradise in the eyes of many bloc inhabitants—and an odious heretic to orthodox Marxists. Market socialism, Yugoslav style, entails worker management of the state-owned industries, through councils directly elected by the employees of each business enterprise. In agriculture, over 85 per cent of the country's land has reverted to private ownership since the collectivization drive was abandoned in 1953.

While Yugoslavia's Communist party retains its political monopoly, a considerable amount of free policy debate is encouraged among its rank-and-file members (over a million in 1967), and some autonomy is allowed to the nation's parliament and judiciary. Tito himself has enjoyed the status of popular national hero ever since his partisans liberated Yugoslavia from the Nazis. His country remains a tantalizing model, so near and yet so far, for aspiring national Communists. Not one has approached Yugoslavia's across-the-board autonomy.

An Erratic Record

To date, the record of autonomy in the bloc countries has been wildly uneven. Few leaders have seen fit to test more than one major new approach at a time, letting other areas languish.

Bulgaria's premier and party chief, Todor Zhivkov, has concentrated on economic expansion and reform, and on attracting Western tourists to spend their hard currency at his country's Black Sea resorts. Tourist revenues, as well as newly discovered deposits of oil and natural gas, are aiding industrial development in a country which until recently was noted chiefly for its yogurt and attar of roses.

Bulgaria's ultraconservative political system has been characterized as "Stalinism without terror." Zhivkov once confided to an interviewer: "I am known for being bound to the Soviet Union in life and death." But the Bulgarians have long been bound by culture and custom to their big Slav brothers next door and are no less accustomed to authoritarian rule. Few appear restive under their current regime.

Poland is unique as a renegade from reform. Twelve years ago the Poles, under their new party secretary Wladyslaw Gomulka, were rejoicing in the freedoms they had won in the peaceful "palace revolution" of October 1956. But a hardening of the liberal arteries gradually set in. Today Gomulka rigidly treads the Moscow line abroad, represses criticism at home and neglects a stagnant economy while he fights to hold party control from other power-hungry hard-liners.

Hungary witnessed a reversal of the Polish trend. Its revolution of November 1956 was anything but peaceful, as Soviet tanks smashed into Budapest and the world shuddered at the agony of the Freedom Fighters. No sane observer of the tragedy would have predicted that within a decade (a) the Hungarians would be tranquilly living under a liberalized Communist regime, apparently letting bygones be bygones; and (b) their liberal Communist leader would be none other than János Kádár, the puppet installed by the Russians amid the ruins of the 1956 revolt.

The colorless Kádár has responded to his countrymen's love of comfort and color by encouraging higher living standards ("goulash communism") as well as arts, amusements and tourism—the latter mostly to and from nearby Vienna. Under his pragmatic creed, "Who is not against us [the Communist party] is with us," non-Communists enjoy the same job and promotion opportunities as party members.

But Kádár is no radical reformer. He waited until January 1968 to test a decentralized "New Economic Model," which has been making modest progress since then. In foreign affairs he obediently follows the Russians—to the point of sending Hungarian troops along with them last August against his Czechoslovak friends.

East Germany has been the bloc's boldest pioneer in economic reform. Party boss Walter Ulbricht took his cue for it, as he does for everything, from the Russians—in this case from the liberal economist Yevsey Liberman, father of Russia's own fledgling market socialism.

In 1963 "Libermanism" was introduced in the GDR, which had inherited a sizable industrial base from pre-World War II days. Today even West Germans acknowledge the success of Ulbricht's "little economic miracle." His country now ranks as the fifth industrial power in Europe, with the highest standard of living in the Communist world.

Politically, Ulbricht remains an old-style Stalinist. Since his people were sealed into East Germany by the Berlin wall in 1961, he has tempered some of his police-state tactics. But the GDR, alone of the bloc states, depends on Soviet power for its very survival as a territorial entity.

No serious observer doubts that, given a free choice, the seventeen million East Germans would vote overwhelmingly for reunion with their West German brethren. Their sense of separate nationhood thus remains dim at best. And Ulbricht, of all Eastern Europe's leaders, can least afford any national-Communist behavior not blessed by his Moscow masters.

Rumania is, so far, the bloc's biggest nuisance to Moscow in international matters. Party chief and President Nicolae Ceausescu has been aptly dubbed "Gaullescu." . . .

Rumania is the only bloc member which has stubbornly refused to take sides in the Sino-Soviet and Arab-Israeli conflicts. It was the first (in January 1967) to establish full diplomatic ties with West Germany.

In 1963 Ceausescu's predecessor, Gheorghe Gheorghiu-Dej, wrecked Soviet plans for the integration of the bloc economies by rejecting the inferior role of raw-materials supplier assigned to Rumania. Since then, Bucharest has relied less on Comecon, more on Western Europe, for trade and aid in building up its industrial base. And since 1964 the Rumanians have reiterated, loud and clear, the inalienable right of every Communist party to pursue its own independent and sovereign course.

At home, however, Ceausescu's course is far less adventurous. The heavy hand of the central planners is clamped on the economy, prodding steel and other heavy industry at the expense of consumer goods. The Communist party reserves the role of rebel for itself; for its Rumanian subjects, few freedoms are tolerated.

Freedom, as the Western democracies understand it, is by definition inconsistent with single-party dictatorship. What some Communist regimes have been able to offer their citizens is relative freedom to enjoy the pleasures of private life and to exert some influence on public policy. But one regime has gone further. Alone among the bloc's national Communists, the Czechoslovaks—for a few unforgettable months . . . [in 1968]—dared to flirt openly with democracy.

Challenge to the West

Has the cold war heated up again? . . .

Anxiety in Western circles has been aroused not only by the actual attack on Czechoslovakia. The latter provoked universal shock and anger in the West but, in itself, posed no physical threat beyond the Soviet "sphere of influence." . . . Adding to Western apprehensions have been:

1. A new strategic balance of forces in Central Europe between NATO and the Warsaw Pact—to the latter's advantage—now that six to eight additional Soviet divisions appear to be permanently camped along the West German border.

2. Thinly veiled Soviet threats against Rumania, Yugoslavia and West Germany in the wake of the Czechoslovak invasion. Many observers interpret Moscow's saber-rattling at Bonn as a psychological tactic (a) to divert Eastern European attention away from Soviet behavior in Czechoslovakia toward the lingering specter of German militarism, and (b) to discourage Bonn's commercial and diplomatic courtship of Eastern Europe, which it is feared could "encircle" East Germany and weaken Comecon.

3. General uncertainty and uneasiness (with the fear of nuclear Armageddon never absent) over the Russians' intentions toward the world at large.

From their recent behavior, should we expect them to pursue a capricious and militant foreign policy, with its incalculable dangers to world peace—and, necessarily, the death of détente?

Or should we take Moscow at its word (to Washington) that it considers its intervention in Czechoslovakia strictly a family affair, and that its interest in discussing disarmament and other cooperative projects with the West is in no way diminished?

Gentleman's Agreement?

Even if we adopt the second view, a major moral issue remains. Moscow's treatment of Prague was a flagrant violation of the UN Charter, the Warsaw Pact's explicit recognition of its members' national sovereignty, and every precept of international law and morality. Must the international community stand by and let the Russians act with impunity against Czechoslovakia (or any unruly ally), simply because the victim belongs to the Communist family and has no other allies committed to come to its aid?

Is there, moreover, a gentleman's agreement between the superpowers that neither will interfere in the other's "sphere of influence"?

Washington has categorically denied making any such deals with Moscow, at the 1945 Yalta Conference or any other time, and very few observers (among them [former] French President de Gaulle) have maintained the contrary. Yet both capitals, in the interests of peace, have respected the status quo in Europe—the present balance of NATO, Warsaw Pact and neutral powers—by refraining from efforts to change it by force. Some observers insist that there has in practice been a tacit agreement that neither the United States nor the U.S.S.R. will poach in the other's treaty preserve.

If true, does this mean that Russia can count on the tacit acquiescence of the United States whenever it chooses to play the rogue elephant in its own preserve—Hungary in 1956, Czechoslovakia in 1968, perhaps Rumania one day?

Of course, argues one school—as long as the United States is unwilling to risk World War III to stop the Russians. Nothing less than the prospect of direct U.S. military intervention can be expected to deter them. When they feel their vital Eastern European interests are at stake, they will certainly not be deterred by moral indignation in Washington, the UN and other centers of "world opinion."

Not necessarily, retorts another school. The Russians are also aware of their vital stake in world peace and East-West coexistence. Witness Soviet Ambassador Dobrynin's hasty call on President Johnson the moment the invasion of Czechoslovakia began, to assure him that the Soviet-led offensive would go no further.

The President's later warning to Moscow not to "unleash the dogs of war" against Rumania may or may not have helped to spare that country from a similar fate. But in the opinion of many critics, Washington should have joined other Western capitals and the UN in issuing loud, unequivocal warnings against intervention during the tense weeks before the Soviet attack on Prague. At the very least, we could have given pause to the Kremlin militants and strengthened the bargaining position of the Kremlin moderates.

Moreover, say these critics, there are effective ways to impress our views on the Russians—short of a military move, stronger than moral censure—which might have been suggested to them. . . .

Suspended Bridge Building

The Western reaction to August 21 [the date of the Soviet move into Czechoslovakia] ranged from minor gestures of disapproval to major delays on détente measures:

The United States postponed several bridge-building projects with Poland and the Soviet Union which were then pending: cultural tours, implementation of the U.S.-U.S.S.R. consular treaty, etc. (As for American trade with the Comecon countries, it has never been large: a total of $372 million in 1967, of which 40 per cent was with Poland, 27 per cent with Russia, 12 per cent with Czechoslovakia.)

West Germany and a number of other nonnuclear nations indicated their strong reluctance to sign the nuclear nonproliferation treaty sponsored by both superpowers. In the

United States, the signed treaty was shelved by the Senate and still awaits ratification.

The NATO allies, confronted with the new strategic balance in Europe, gave up hope and talk of a "mutual reduction of forces" for the foreseeable future. . . .

Plans for bilateral Soviet-American talks on reducing arsenals of strategic nuclear missiles were put on ice for the time being. (Announcement of a Johnson-Kosygin summit meeting to launch the talks had been scheduled for the very day Czechoslovakia was invaded.) Meanwhile, the superpower arms race continues to spiral: Washington is going ahead with a new $5.5 billion antiballistic missile system.

Reappraising East-West Relations

The . . . year's events . . . unquestionably added fuel to a long-simmering controversy: What policies should the United States (in concert, as far as possible, with the other Western allies) pursue toward the Soviet bloc? Three broad policy lines are being debated:

Containment with minimal contact? The Czechoslovak crisis has reinvigorated this tough cold-war approach based on nuclear deterrence, NATO preparedness and the fewest possible commercial and cultural "bridges." The Soviet empire—all of it—remains our totalitarian adversary. Why should we reward any of its component regimes with our exports, tariff preferences, tourist dollars, etc. for what are at most superficial differences in Communist behavior? (Czechoslovakia is, after all, a supplier of arms to North Vietnam.)

Instead, we should step up our propaganda campaign to the captive peoples of Eastern Europe. And we must strengthen our Western alliance, using it to exploit all strains in the Eastern European alliance until the Soviet bloc breaks apart and Europe (particularly Germany) can be reunited in freedom.

Selective coexistence? The monolithic Soviet bloc has long been a myth. The Russians can still maintain its frontiers and a considerable degree of political conformity by force. But they cannot prevent its national Communists from seeking pragmatic solutions to their practical economic needs —and ever-greater contacts with the advanced technological societies of the West.

Little by little, with the freer movement of goods and ideas and people between the two halves of Europe, a freer internal climate will begin to prevail in the eastern half. The bloc is less likely to explode into pieces which the West can pick up than to evolve, very slowly and unevenly, toward reunion with the rest of Europe.

Thus our dealings with Eastern Europe should be selective. We must try to promote further progress among the independent "good guys" (Rumania, Czechoslovakia) with our trade and other exchanges, and withhold them from the "bad guys" (East Germany, Poland) to weaken their resistance to reform.

When the Soviet Union is on good behavior we should build bridges there as well. However, when it misbehaves we must take care to distinguish between ceremonial contacts and our mutual stake in survival. It is one thing to rebuke the Russians for Czechoslovakia by canceling summit conferences and symphony concerts. It is another to punish them and ourselves by renouncing talks with them on such life-and-death matters as nuclear arms control.

Bridge-building with the entire bloc? In this conciliatory view, the Czechoslovak episode is no more than a temporary setback to an inevitable process of reform. In every country of the Soviet bloc there are forces—among the youth and the professional and technical elite if not the present rulers— moving to liberalize their Communist system and reconcile it with non-Communist Europe. The eloquent plea for such a policy which was issued . . . by the eminent Russian physicist Andrei Sakharov testifies to its appeal in the most prestigious circles of Soviet society.

We, for our part, should encourage this evolution throughout Communist Europe by eliminating as many restrictions as possible on travel, nonstrategic trade, cultural and scientific exchanges, and even investment.

TOWARD A NEW PARTNERSHIP WITH EUROPE [3]

The United States and Europe need each other. This is more widely accepted today on both sides of the Atlantic than ever before. What is at issue between us is the form that our relationship should take during a period of change and adjustment.

Change is an uncomfortable thing. It has an unsettling effect. It is easier to see what one has given up than what one will gain. But change is also an inescapable feature of life. There was a time when Europe felt that it needed us much more than we needed it. Indeed, in the immediate postwar period Europe was totally dependent on us, both for its security and for the economic means to make its recovery. Dependence creates a special intimacy, a relationship of its own—and generally not one of a healthy and enduring nature. But just as these circumstances have changed, so, inevitably, must our relationship with Europe change.

We can, with all modesty, be justly proud of our record during this period. We not only rose to the immediate challenge, but also anticipated the need to put our relationship with Europe on a more enduring basis. Secretary of State James F. Byrnes held out the hand of friendship to the Germans . . . in September 1946, and General George C. Marshall to all Europeans in June 1947. The concept of a partnership between the United States and Europe was enunciated by President Kennedy in Philadelphia on July 4, 1962, and became the guiding principle of our European policy.

This is why we have consistently supported plans to strengthen Europe and give it greater unity. Through the cooperative military organization of NATO, we and the Europeans created a counterpoise to Soviet power that has pre-

[3] From article by George C. McGhee, former U.S. ambassador to West Germany. *Saturday Review*. 52:16-18. Mr. 8, '69. Copyright 1969 Saturday Review, Inc. Reprinted by permission.

served the peace. We welcomed the Monnet and Schuman proposals [for European integration]. We supported the plans for a European Defense Community. We have encouraged the creation of the European Community, and also its enlargement to include the United Kingdom and other eligible countries. We have also encouraged a widening of the scope of Community action, moving ultimately into the political arena.

Some may say that we acted on occasion with such excessive zeal that we imparted a strong American flavor to what must be essentially a European effort. But if there was an excess of zeal, it was in the service of a good cause. We saw that Europe could in this way become comparable to us. This not only would permit Europe to play a larger world role, but would have a salutary effect on the unhealthy consequences of our present disparity.

Although not all of these plans for Europe have come to full fruition, considerable progress has been made. Traditional rivalries between the countries of Western Europe have been damped down. The economies of the Common Market countries . . . have burgeoned while becoming inextricably bound together. As a result, the people of continental Europe have acquired a new feeling of togetherness as "Europeans." There are the beginnings of a "European" nationalism. There is a growing conviction that Europe should once again determine its own destiny and assume a leading role in world efforts. Thus, while we do not as yet have a Europe which "speaks with one voice," there is a more independent and self-reliant Europe that is proud of its accomplishments and faces the future with confidence.

The feeling that our relations with Europe today are not as close as they were in the fifties derives, I believe, more from the fact that our relations have changed than why or how they have changed. It need not be disturbing. It need not, as is often charged, represent neglect on our part—the subordination of Europe to the Vietnam war. It need not, on the other hand, represent a deliberate effort on the part of Europeans to distance themselves from us.

What is sometimes taken to be an anti-American sentiment on the part of Europeans does not necessarily reflect a desire to disassociate themselves from us, but rather to reorient themselves with respect to us. Many Europeans wish to get out from under what they consider has been an undue American influence and to get alongside of that influence. They do not wish to give us up. Experience has shown them, as well as us, that we can and must cooperate with each other.

If this is so, what, then, should be the model for America's evolving relationship with Europe? First, it cannot be one of dominance by us—even if we wished it. One view is that the United States would, within an informal grouping, impinge directly upon the other countries of the Atlantic world—and they on us and each other. In the end, we would represent, with all of our inequalities, one big happy family with us the head. This might be pleasing for us, but it is not likely to be so for the Europeans. Moreover, European unity has gone too far to turn back.

Our Government, on the other hand, has long hoped that once Europe becomes unified, a relationship would develop between us which we have described as a "partnership." This term has never been fully defined, but it is assumed that it would involve, as in a business partnership, a sharing of the risks and responsibilities—as well as the rewards—of our joint efforts. We would expect to treat each other as equals, particularly since a united Europe would in fact be our equal. We see no conflict between the two concepts: European Community and Atlantic Community.

But what about the basic assumption underlying this concept of partnership: that Europe will move toward greater political unity? The outlook at the moment, it must be admitted, is inconclusive. Although our support for a larger Europe is well known, there is really little that we can do about it. The hopes of some Europeans that greater economic cohesion would automatically lead to greater political unity have not been realized.

Indeed, the success of the European Community on the economic side, and a growing readiness among its members to accord purely economic concessions to . . . [other European] countries, may have relieved some of the pressure for advances—requiring difficult and unpleasant decisions—on the political side. . . .

On the other hand, strong unifying forces remain that make the ultimate outlook not unpromising. Powerful groups, including not only government leaders but intellectuals, youth, and the European labor movement, strongly support a unified Europe. We must remember, too, that the Community is not the only focus for unity in Europe. There is also Strasbourg (the Council of Europe) and the WEU (Western European Union), and the vast private sector, which moves in a similar direction.

We must, however, rid ourselves of the idea that Europe must become fully unified before the form of its ultimate relationship with us can begin to unfold. It may be useful to think of U.S.-European relations not in terms of two pillars standing on opposite sides of the Atlantic, but in terms of two trains generally moving in the same direction along roughly parallel tracks. Our train gives the outward appearance of uniformity, while the European train consists of a variety of cars with the possibility that others may be added. This difference may, however, not be so important as the fact that we are headed in the same direction, and at comparable speeds so that one can keep up with the other.

Indeed, we in America may in the past have been understandably overrigid in our concept of the way Europe should be unified. Our preference for a federal approach is in all probability derived from our own historical development. There may, however, be other avenues toward unity which could yield better results because they are more compatible with Europe's own traditions. It may be that European unity will not come about at all as we have anticipated—i.e., through a dramatic political act at the top—but rather through inundation from below. It may come through an increasing emergence into the European fabric of the bureaucracy of the Common Market and other international institutions, and of the further encroachment of the private sector.

Much of the business of Europe today is directed by the eight thousand members of the staff of the European Community. Intra-European trade is now not a national but a European Community matter. In external trade the states have abdicated their sovereignty to the Community, which acts for all of the Six. Increasingly, other fields heretofore reserved for national action, such as financial policy, are becoming matters for Community decision.

Taking into account other intergovernmental activities organized on a broader basis, such as those assumed by NATO, the OECD (Organization for Economic Cooperation and Development), the GATT (General Agreement on Tariffs and Trade), the IMF (International Monetary Fund), and the United Nations and its subsidiary organizations, there remains a decreasing residue of matters which are the subject of purely national action. Indeed, the time will come when Europe will find that the tip of the national iceberg is very small—involving only the highest policy decisions—in comparison with that greater portion that is submerged in international bureaucratic channels.

At the same time, Europe is also becoming more closely knit in the private sector. This process was sparked by carefully placed plant investments by American companies, which were the first to take advantage of the Common Market by creating integrated European industries. A beginning has been made, however, on purely European mergers and investments across country lines, and on closer cooperation between the industrial groupings of the members of the Six. [See "Europe's Merger Boom Thunders a Lot Louder," in Section II above.] Cooperation in Europewide television, road networks [see "EEC Makes Headway on Highways" in Section II, above], and airlines, and increasing personal contacts through tourism, sports, and cultural cooperation are all having their unifying effect.

The same is true, however, of the evolution of the Atlantic Community, which hopefully will provide nourishment for the developing partnership between the United States and Europe. NATO is an Atlantic-focused organization that generates a high degree of "Atlantic" cooperation, not just in the military but in political and other fields. An example is the decision reached at the fall 1967 NATO meeting in Brussels that the organization would play a significantly larger political role.

Atlantic cohesion is also developing at a rapid pace in the private sectors. In science and technology there already exists an Atlantic Community. Atomic scientists from Karlsruhe are equally at home at Los Alamos—just as scientists of other fields move readily from Oxford to Berkeley. Trade and investment between Europe and America have reached unprecedented heights. U.S. direct investment in Europe recently stood at $17.9 billion; combined exports and imports between us add up to the same amount. The great international companies, whether domiciled in North America or Europe, are owned in both places. They are managed by internationalists. Their goals and policies do not know national boundaries. In the aggregate, they constitute one of the strongest of the "Atlantic" forces.

The Atlantic nations are also working together in an effort to solve the most basic world problem: lessening the gap between the industrialized and the developing countries. The existence of this gap introduces an element of tension in the world which, if not relieved, could become a serious threat to European, as well as to our own, security.

There are other ties too numerous to mention—the press, television, the theater and graphic arts—which are developing in large part on an Atlantic basis. Through tourism, the intermingling of individuals in fraternal and professional organizations, and in countless other ways, the Atlantic world is increasingly being bound together. These myriad ties constitute the warp and woof of our common Atlantic fabric—quite immune from day-to-day political vicissitudes.

At this particular stage, we should not, I believe, worry too much about whether the European Community is getting ahead of the Atlantic Community—or vice versa—or whether they are in phase or in conflict. They are both happening simultaneously under our very noses, in the only real way they can—as a result of the natural interplay of governmental and private forces. If one gets temporarily ahead, the other will catch up. The main thing is that they are going ahead together—and in the same direction.

In the meantime, much as we wish the Europeans would do more to help us in carrying out the manifold defensive tasks of the free world, there is little that we can do to hasten evolution in European thinking in this regard. Our best line is to make clear that we cannot indefinitely bear the present disproportionate share of free world defense; that we expect Europe to play a greater European and world role; and that, when they make such a decision, we will welcome them as full partners.

This evolution would be greatly accelerated if we could make a greater effort, through frank discussions with our European friends, to arrive at a closer common assessment of world problems that deserve our primary attention. In doing so, we must be prepared to adapt our views to theirs, as well as to attempt to influence them.

Perhaps Europeans will be aroused to take a defensive stand outside of their own continent only in the event of some unfortunate new cataclysm directly affecting them. A threat to the North African littoral world, for example, would be too close to home for them to ignore. Hopefully, however, before that time comes, the Europeans will come to see it as being in their own interest to join us in the only goal worthy of our joint efforts: the longer-range task of making of the free world an edifice that is not only unassailable by enemies from without, but one within which men can build a society worthy of free people.

WEST GERMANY AND POLAND [4]

Despite the drag of history, Poland today is ready, willing and even eager to come to terms with its longtime *bête noire,* West Germany.

This is the inescapable conclusion after . . . conversations with numerous leading Poles, official and unofficial, who make or influence policy or who are in a position to know the attitude of the ruling Communist leadership.

Every sign is that Poland was given the green light at . . . [a] gathering in Moscow of the Warsaw Pact nations. The sigh of relief here is immense.

Officially, of course, there is caution. Indeed as is usually the case in advance of critical negotiations there are cries that West German Chancellor Willy Brandt is backsliding from his startling shift in his own nation's past position.

Moscow Watching

It is evident that the negotiations will be difficult. It is evident that Moscow will be watching every move. It is evident that the Poles are worried that somehow the East Germans, wary of rapprochement between their neighbors to East and West, may somehow erect an impassable roadblock.

But the tone in Warsaw today is definitely positive. And the detailed discussion one hears of the individual pieces of the puzzle that must be put together strongly bespeaks compromise. Poles in a position to know say there is, today, a slim majority in the Politburo for normalization of Polish-West German relations.

It was . . . [a] speech of the Communist party secretary, Wladyslaw Gomulka, the initial Polish opening to the West, which set the current train of events in motion. This came

[4] From "Poles Eager to Start Talks with Bonn to Normalize Ties," article by Chalmers M. Roberts, correspondent. *International Herald Tribune.* p 6. D. 15, '69. Reprinted by permission.

after the Gustav Husak regime took over in Prague, marking the "normalization" in Czechoslovakia that the Kremlin had demanded. Mr. Brandt's September [1969] election and his foreign minister's October offer of talks "on the basis of what Wladyslaw Gomulka said on May 17 [1969]" made negotiations possible. The Poles say they expect them to begin early ... [in 1970].

Thus Poland ... is permitted to act within the Brezhnev doctrine, which is the Kremlin's unilateral limitation on the sovereignty of its fellow Communist states. It is named for the Russian Communist party chief, Leonid I. Brezhnev.

Some outsiders here argue that the Polish regime's long-time dependence on the West German bogeyman has been found to be no longer necessary to control the population. They reason that there was no vast public feeling against ... [the 1968] anti-Semitic campaign, that Poland helped invade Czechoslovakia with only minimal public reaction and that ... [the 1968] student outburst failed to catch fire.

Strong Hold

Hence, this reasoning goes, the regime found its hold on the public stronger than it realized. The Czechoslovak book was closed. The Soviet Union, worried about its China problem, was more amenable to Eastern deals with the West. Mr. Brandt provided an opening. And so the old anti-German bogeyman could be downplayed if not exactly ended.

However, Poles today say that the anti-German feeling, from the Hitlerite crimes and the long period of public indoctrination, is still so strong that the regime must move warily.

A Polish opinion poll, taken ... after Mr. Brandt came to power but never published, investigated the public attitude to normalizing Polish-West German relations. About 99 per cent said that it should not be done unless Germany recognized Poland's Western border, known as the Oder-Neisse line. But 60 per cent said that there should not be normalization unless West Germany recognized East Germany as a sovereign state.

Examination Necessary

It is necessary to examine the details of the Oder-Neisse line problem, the recognition issue, the question of Poland's hoped-for credits from West Germany and Poland's attitude toward the Communist bloc's proposed European security conference and the related issue of mutual reduction of conventional arms in Central Europe.

Oder-Neisse: This is the overwhelmingly important issue for the Polish regime. The aim is to end forever all West German or Western talk that some day the pre-World War II border farther to the east might be reestablished despite Russia's guarantee of the Oder-Neisse line.

Mr. Brandt has refused a total recognition of the line on the grounds that the 1945 Potsdam Agreement by the United States, the Soviet Union, Britain and France reserves a final settlement of Germany's borders for a peace treaty. The official Polish position . . . is that Mr. Brandt should ask the four whether his nation now has sufficient sovereignty to sign. It is pointed out that Moscow agrees and that Paris already has recognized the line. Just what Washington would say, if Mr. Brandt were really to ask approval, is impossible to say but such a request would be difficult to refuse if other conditions favored an agreement.

How hard Poland will push this point one cannot estimate. Some Poles say, however—with some evidence—that they do not expect it to be pushed to a breaking point and, in fact, that agreement on the Oder-Neisse is now simply a problem of finding language acceptable to Bonn and Warsaw which skirts that problem.

Recognition of East Germany: The official Polish formulation is that West Germany—the FRG—must recognize "the existence of the German Democratic Republic—DDR—as a sovereign and fully legal German state." The Moscow summit formulation was somewhat more elastic. It called on all

nations in "the interests of peace and security" to "establish
equal relations with the German Democratic Republic on
the basis of international law."

Mr. Brandt has said that the Federal Republic of Germany would never recognize the DDR as a separate nation
and he has countered with the new formulation that there
are "two German states in one nation."

Solution Seen

Very high personages among the Poles, asked about this
formulation, pointed out that the constitutions of both Germanys declare each to be a part of a German state. This appeared to reflect a feeling, though it was not so stated, that
Mr. Brandt had cleverly created a formula on which could
be constructed a satisfactory solution.

Another Polish suggestion, on a lower level, is also new.
This is that both German states could be admitted to the
United Nations, thus affording a form of international recognition to East Germany without the necessity of West Germany establishing the kind of direct diplomatic relations
that are normal between sovereign states. Bonn's reaction to
this idea is unknown here, though there are informed hints
that it might be possible.

Because of these complexities Poles of importance say
that recognition is basically an issue between the two German states and that resolution of the Oder-Neisse problem
will not have to await settlement on recognition. Whether
the Russians and East Germans agree may be something else
again.

Polish-West German trade: The common assumption
here is that Poland is seeking a West German line of credit
totaling about $550 million over a five year period. The figure recently has surfaced in Bonn where trade talks have
just been resumed. The Polish plan is to pay for credits with
the products of the plants they build or with copper.

To meet its ambitious 1971-75 five-year-plan goals, Poland envisages purchases in the West of around $1 billion to $1.5 billion. Poland plans what is called "selective and intensive" development, meaning emphasis on such fields as electronics, petrochemicals, electrical machinery and machinery in general. The Soviet Union and Eastern Europe alone cannot meet such needs. Of the Western nations only West Germany seems prepared to do so.

Skeptical Specialists

Some Poles, aware of this massive West German economic leverage on political issues, speak bravely of such alternate capital sources as Britain, France and Japan. But the economic specialists are highly skeptical.

Both Poland and West Germany publicly separate the trade and credit issue from the political issues. But Mr. Brandt is highly conscious of his economic leverage and doubtless intends to use it.

European Security Conference and Arms Limitation: In earlier years, Poland put forward the Rapacki and Gomulka plans calling for either a freezing or reduction of nuclear arms on the territories of Central European states, proposals designed to get American nuclear weapons out of West Germany.

These ideas have largely disappeared from Polish statements. . . . The Poles now explain that the West German signature on the nuclear nonproliferation treaty has altered the picture and that currently new studies are under way here to find new formulations. It also is hinted that Moscow is awaiting a clearer picture of the outcome of the strategic arms talks in Helsinki with the United States.

Possibilities Noted

The Polish response to the recent NATO foreign ministers' call for mutual force reductions in Europe is that it may offer possibilities later on. [The Western allies, meanwhile, have been talking of a unilateral reduction of their NATO forces.—Ed.]

Poland formally favors the European security conference of all European nations. And Poles repeat the Moscow statement that there is "no objection" to American and Canadian participation. But this seems to be said by rote now that bilateral talks already have begun between Moscow and Bonn and are impending between Moscow and Warsaw with some sort of talks also likely between the two German states.

Furthermore, Warsaw knows that the United States strongly backs the bilateral approach, as well as the multilateral approach, on the Berlin issue, and simply will not now agree to a general conference. The Poles add that there might be a series of conferences but they are rather indefinite about it.

GERMANY LOOKS EAST: RESHAPING EUROPE [5]

The greatest danger that I see in the present situation is that Germany may throw in her lot with Bolshevism and place her resources, her brains, her vast organizing power at the disposal of the revolutionary fanatics whose dream is to conquer the world for Bolshevism by force of arms.

Thus wrote British Prime Minister David Lloyd George at the Versailles peace conference fifty years ago. And his words proved prophetic. For just three years later, Germany and Russia negotiated a secret rapprochement at Rapallo—and the way was open to military collaboration between the Reichswehr and the Red Army. Observing the current warming trend between Bonn and Moscow, there were some in Europe who were muttering . . . about "another Rapallo." That kind of reflection was, of course, scare talk. Yet even though it often exaggerated the case to the point of paranoia, widespread concern over the current West German-Soviet flirtation revealed a profound truth: if carried far enough, it will reshape the political map of Europe.

For the time being, the two chief cartographers in this exercise are Soviet Foreign Minister Andrei Gromyko and

[5] From article in *Newsweek*. 74:33-4. O. 22, '69. Copyright Newsweek, Inc., 1969. Reprinted by permission.

West German Ambassador to Moscow Helmut Allardt. Iron-
ically, . . . Allardt was forced to cool his heels in the Soviet
capital for more than a year before the Soviets paid him
serious attention. . . . Finally, . . . when he received a telephone message that Gromyko was ready to begin immediate
bilateral talks on a mutual renunciation-of-force treaty,
Allardt's patience paid off. In a flurry of diplomatic activity,
he and Gromyko met twice in quick succession at . . . the
Soviet Foreign Ministry for the most significant exchange of
views between West Germany and the Soviet Union since
the end of World War II. The specific subjects that the two
men discussed remained a guarded secret. Indeed, the very
notion of Russians and West Germans sitting amicably
around a conference table in downtown Moscow was so politically explosive in the Soviet Union that Tass, the official
Soviet news agency, never once reported the existence of the
talks.

   Contacts: Russians were also kept in the dark about West
Germany's contacts with Moscow's Communist neighbors.
. . . At a Warsaw Pact meeting in Moscow, the Soviet Union
gave the East Europeans a green light to begin their own
bilateral negotiations with the Federal Republic. Poland was
the first to take advantage of the opportunity, resuming talks
with Bonn on increased trade and technical cooperation.
Then the Hungarians announced that Foreign Trade Minister Jozsef Biro would be arriving in West Germany early
[in 1970] to negotiate a trade agreement between Bonn and
Budapest. Even Czechoslovakia—which, in the wake of the
Soviet-led invasion, has good reason to be wary of cozying
up to Bonn—suggested that it would "welcome and carefully
consider" an offer from West Germany to renounce the
Munich Agreement—the 1938 pact that ceded the Sudeten-
land to the Nazis.

   What most East European countries hoped to extract
from West Germany was obvious enough—trade and technical exchange agreements to modernize their economies. But
the motives behind the Soviet desire for a rapprochement

with Bonn went well beyond basic economics to the murky area of international geopolitics. To begin with, the Kremlin leaders viewed closer contacts with West Germany as one step in the direction of the European Security Conference that they have so insistently called for in recent months— presumably for the purpose of confirming the status quo in East Europe, at a time when Moscow feels increasingly threatened by the Communist Chinese. In this regard, a meeting . . . in Warsaw between U.S. and Chinese diplomats to discuss the resumption of full-scale ambassadorial talks between the two countries could have done little to alleviate Soviet fears that Peking may receive wider acceptance by the world community in the near future.

Motive: But an equally important motive behind the Soviet desire to improve the East-West atmosphere was its long-standing twin goal of dividing the United States from its NATO allies and disrupting West European economic integration. By matching West German Chancellor Willy Brandt's *Ost-Politik* with a *West-Politik* of its own, the Soviet Union seemed to be showing its willingness to dismantle the delicate balance of terror that has been the basic cement of both the NATO and the Warsaw Pact alliances for two decades. And the rebuff that the United States received at the meeting of NATO foreign ministers in Brussels . . . when it failed to convince its allies to include a denunciation of the invasion of Czechoslovakia in the final communiqué, may have been the first sign of the effectiveness of Moscow's strategy.

Whatever the long-range goals of the Kremlin leaders, their timing was impeccable. For since the naming of Willy Brandt as Chancellor of the Federal Republic . . . they have been dealing with a man who is an imaginative advocate of dismantling the East-West confrontation in Europe. In the view of most observers, Brandt's *Ost-Politik* seemed motivated primarily by a desire to improve relations with East Germany. Even now, however, East German Communist Party boss Walter Ulbricht insists that, unless Bonn recognizes his . . . regime, no reconciliation between East and West Germany is possible. And while this is exactly what all postwar West German leaders have refused to do, many of Brandt's political opponents think that his *Ost-Politik* will ultimately lead to just such a move. . . .

The nervousness with which Brandt's domestic opponents view his policy is shared to a large degree by his foreign friends. At the NATO conference, Secretary of State William Rogers expressed the Nixon Administration's reservations about the usefulness of a European Security Conference at the current juncture—and during a visit to Paris last week for talks with French officials, Rogers warned America's allies against falling into "a false sense of détente." Certainly, the French government of President Georges Pompidou needed no such advice. For although Charles de Gaulle himself advocated a bilateral approach to East-West rapprochement, France was having second thoughts about the wisdom of this course now that West Germany had taken the diplomatic initiative. "I have always maintained," said a former Gaullist official, "that unless we created Europe in the sixties, we would no longer have any control over Germany in the seventies."

Ties: No one was more aware of the dangers inherent in Bonn's present policy initiatives than Willy Brandt himself. Too sophisticated a politician to have the wool pulled over his eyes by the Russians, Brandt has repeatedly stated that he has no intention of sacrificing his country's ties with the West in the pursuit of détente with the East. During his years as mayor of West Berlin and foreign minister of the Federal Republic, he learned to approach the Soviet Union with caution and with more than a fleeting over-the-shoulder glance at his allies. Indeed, Brandt's point of view seemed to be summed up well by West German Defense Minister Helmut Schmidt, who told the West European Union Assembly in Paris . . . [October 1969]: "It would be sheer folly if one attempted to conduct one's policy toward the East from any other basis than that of firm Western solidarity."

THE MAKING OF EUROPE [6]

What will become of our Europe? Better, what can it become? Better still, what can we make of it, and what do we want to make of it?

We can by no means merely extrapolate from the past; we must also try to see something basically new—and demand it, too—with the aim of preserving and enriching the life of those who live in Europe. For cultures naturally consist of people, those now alive, those to come and those who have left some evidence of their lives—their creations or their failures—in objective works, whether of a material, intellectual or social character.

Some Initial Questions

To start with, we must deal with the following question: What do we mean by Europe in this context? What can Europe actually mean today? Is it more than a geographical term; is it a unit of socio-political significance? And if so, of what kind?

Indeed, the inhabitants of Europe have never seen themselves as members of a unit, hence they have never—sociologically and psychologically speaking—been Europeans. Particular antagonisms have always outweighed integrating solidarity, even when the Turks stood before Constantinople in the middle of the fifteenth century and, two hundred years later, before Vienna. The Europeans have shown an incomparably "productive" fantasy in creating occasions, slogans, social myths and other justifications for their aggressions, persecutions and exterminations. The power of the polis; the pasture rights of a valley; the market rights of a small town; a landlord's right of exploitation; a sovereign's right of succession; an emperor's right of tenure; the coronation rights of the Pope; the privileges of patricians; the monopoly rights of guilds; the rights of clerical authorities to send dissenters to the stake or to exterminate them in crusades—all

[6] From article by Richard F. Behrendt, a German authority on international development sociology. *Interplay*. 3:14-19. Ag.-S. '69. Reprinted by permission.

these have served again and again as motives for the destruction of human beings and human welfare. Finally, our times have added to these motives the demand of new classes, newly awakened peoples and races for emancipation and participation in the growing prosperity.

None of the mythic ideas which we use in our attempts at understanding ourselves and in political propaganda inside and outside Europe has ever been a workable social reality, an "integration"—neither Europe, nor the "West," nor Christianity. So far, European self-awareness has never been institutionalized, has never been shaped to unified action, and has not been able to create a solid system of order. The present concept of an "integrated" rump-Europe faces this test as well as a variety of other obstacles.

The Impact of North America

In the past, the European consciousness has had to serve again and again as an ideological slogan and as an attempt to legitimatize the trends toward overseas expansion or toward the continental hegemony of a dynasty or a country, from the Hapsburgs and Spain to Cromwell's and Pitt's England to the France of Louis XIV and Napoleon up (or down) to the German Reich of Wilhelm II and Hitler. During World War II and immediately after it, the consciousness of Europe was partly altered by a Western ideology mainly imparted by the United States. The image of "Western civilization" and that of the "American century" were somewhat hastily and naively fused. Historical symbols and reminiscences were borrowed, rather one-sidedly, from the bourgeois liberal and democratic component of European culture which especially links the United States with its spiritual predecessors in Western Europe.

With this process an astonishing change came temporarily to an end. Originally a revolutionary British colony, North America moved from the principle of self-sufficient isolation, aloof from the "quarrels and intrigues" of European politics, toward its "manifest destiny" as civilizer of the New World under the cloak of the Monroe Doctrine, and then right into its new role of predominance in the "free world"—thereby acting as the protector of non-Communist Europe. It is unavoidable in this context to think of the role the Germans played, compared to that of the rest of the world, in the undoubtedly final weakening of Europe. Not only was Germany to an important degree responsible for the coming about of World War I, and to a decisive degree responsible for World War II, but she also made a particular—if involuntary—contribution to the rise of the United States and the Soviet Union as the leading world powers. The Soviet Union, strengthened and expanded as a result of the defeat of Hitler's Germany, now became the object of the new polemic of Western ideology—of the free world. There has, however, developed a widening gap between the ideology of the free world and that of Europe, as a direct reaction to the U.S. hegemony within the framework of an occidental concept transcending Europe. General de Gaulle's image of a "Europe of Fatherlands"—in distinct contrast to the Anglo-Saxon sphere, which is necessarily oriented overseas—is typical.

Needed: A Concept Free of Ideology

These reflections are only meant to show the necessity in our thinking for a concept of Europe as unideological and politically neutral as possible. If we want to talk of the Europe of today and tomorrow we have to free ourselves from the arbitrary and unstable character of historical and polemical definitions and interpretations. We have to try to develop a concept of Europe which will clarify the problem from a sociological point of view and be socio-politically workable. This concept must be based on the extraordinary part played by certain European countries during the last centuries as centers and dynamos of worldwide change, as well as on the fact that Europe missed its chance to concentrate on this function of its global dimension.

The only valid definition of Europe today must be derived from the following unique achievement: Europe is the place where the modern world was created and where the exploration and penetration of the world originated. Europe opened up the world both economically and in terms of transport. It gave impetus to the organization of the division of labor and the functional integration of the world. It thus produced "mankind" as a—potential, at least—unit of experience and action. Yet even in this respect Europe has never formed a functional unity. The dynamic impulses and achievements have taken place in very different degrees and with geographical shifts—in particular from the south to the northwest, then to the center and to the east. . . . These achievements have not been brought about by unified, co-operative actions, but largely in spite of, or even as part of, rival confrontations—mainly with no awareness of the significance of what was being done.

Often and in all parts of the world there have been territorial and commercial expansion, migrations and resettlements, cross-cultural fertilization. The unique achievement of Europe, however, consists of the creation and dissemination of a new type of culture and society, characterized by dynamism, which proved to be not only an expansive but a democratizing and revolutionary mode of living. It consists of replacing static forms of technology and economy by vigorous ones capable of development. It has replaced hierarchic systems of social stratification based on tradition and sharp hereditary differences by flexible, mobile social systems wherein the individual achievement becomes more and more decisive in establishing social status. It has weakened the monocratic or oligarchic systems of government in favor of democratic ones which correspond—at least in ethical and legal theory and structural form—to the growing demands of the masses for participation in decision making and in the fruits of this dynamic development.

The Revolutionary Consequences of Expansion

This explains why the expansion of Europe across the earth could not be achieved without important changes in power, cultural and property structures. While expanding, European culture had to remodel the non-European territories, even in a revolutionary manner, after its own image. In the beginning, this revolution took place inside those countries by weakening and often overthrowing their traditional value systems and socio-political orders; it continued through the demand of the non-European peoples for emancipation from the hegemony of the West—direct political emancipation or indirect economic emancipation.

This demand for emancipation and the necessity of satisfying it was considerably accelerated by Europe's own suicide attempts—the two world wars . . . and the Western inability to draw constructive conclusions from the results of these wars, thus running at the same time the risk of anarchy. This failure of the European self-consciousness to grasp the significance of the historical moment led to useless and psychologically destructive colonial wars, and to the improvisation of "national" independence for dozens of territories in Asia, Africa and the West Indies which were unprepared for this new form of existence and very often did not even possess the most elementary objective conditions required for it. In other words: European hegemony broke down so hastily and in such an improvised manner because the Europeans had not understood—and still do not understand sufficiently—that their own behavior, their way of life and naturally also their own teachings would necessarily act as provocative images and models with worldwide effects.

Europe discovered the world and shaped it into a functional unity, i.e., into a complex of different though materially, spiritually and socially connected, even interdependent, social structures. Yet it failed to convert them into a unity which would guarantee the survival of its members and protect them from anarchy. Along with its global dynamism, Europe has for the first time shown the realizable possibilities of a form of living worthy of human beings. Yet so far this form of living has been only for the benefit of a comparatively small number of people. The resulting tensions and conflicts cast doubts on the chances of survival not only of Europe but—in the face of the present stage of technology, with its power of absolute destruction—of mankind as a whole.

The Price of Dynamism

Thus we have paid a price for the dynamism of our age. It consists first of all in having had to lose the security of the permanent and familiar; it also consists of the insecurities, uncertainties, fears and instabilities connected with the perpetual breakthrough into the new; it has to do with the difficulties of adjusting psychologically, spiritually and socially to the conditions of life in this new world which European sciences, technology and economy themselves have created and are constantly reshaping.

In large areas of Europe it has become fashionable to swing back and forth between two attitudes. On the one hand, there is an arrogant paternalism accompanied by a dogmatic pedantry concerning the outside world; on the other hand, a deep pessimism with regard to our own possibilities. . . .

Within . . . [a] general feeling of inevitable European decline, still another argument is brought forward by two opposing sides, the conservative nationalists and the revolutionary Marxists. It says that Europeans (or some of them), as "peoples without space," are dependent on overseas colonies, either as markets and areas for settlement or as political support for the "capitalist" system, and that therefore to give up the colonies would mean further decline, certainly the decline of the present European economic system. This assumption was never really justified, and now has completely lost any rational basis; one has only to look at today's Netherlands after the "loss" of Indonesia, at West Germany, Switzerland, Scandinavia—precisely the countries with the highest standard of living in Europe.

Also the "Americanization" of European industries, so often regretted and resented, is not a matter of fate, but the result of a slackening of the dynamic impulse, especially in the entrepreneurial field. This is due partly to the fact that European enterprise has been relatively well off in terms of manpower (thanks to the influx from underdeveloped southern Europe), which seemed to permit European management a more casual attitude toward the encouragement of research for rationalization and mechanization in production and marketing than had been adopted by its American competitors. Generally speaking, I think that Europe is still insufficiently oriented toward the future. New possibilities and requirements are rarely anticipated; instead, Europeans are inclined to let "things turn up" and then to react to them, often too late and therefore inadequately. Thus they sometimes lose out in the race with the more mobile Americans or the Japanese.

A Key Factor: Education

Europe's backwardness is particularly serious when it comes to the question of education, which in many European countries today is still based on long-outdated patterns determined by status thinking. For example, the Esso company has calculated that in 1963 those graduating with a twelve-year full-time school education represented 73 per cent of their age group in the United States compared to only 8 per cent in West Germany. In 1970 the figure will be 80 per cent in the United States but still not more than 8 per cent in West Germany. This habit of sticking to antiquated concepts of social order and structure causes countless difficulties, hindering cooperation between members of different academic disciplines, bureaucratic organizations, national administrations, between schools of different categories, between schools and universities and among the universities themselves. Another manifestation of those outworn patterns is the enduring prejudice against professional mobility, i.e., changing from one profession to another within a lifetime, which is essential in a dynamic economy and society. . . .

A Reluctance to Confront the Future

Europeans have started to think about the future only sporadically. Our "humanities" still deal mostly with what was, very little with what is, and hardly at all with what should be, could be—and may be. This is due not only to methodological scruples—the demand for freedom from value judgments and the impossibility of setting goals for human actions from a scientific point of view—but also to one-sided spiritual ties to the past. There is a reluctance to deal with the problems of the historical loneliness from which we suffer, as well as with the possibilities of the emancipation from history which we must, to some extent, bring about.

A one-sided subordination to the past (or what one likes to imagine as the past), and the feeling of being bound to the historical principle as a determining fate, point to an existential weakness, to a fear of the unknown, of new and larger horizons; fear, also, in the face of alternatives and the necessity of choosing one or the other with full responsibility. All this is a common symptom characteristic of "old" cultures which grew up with authoritarian patterns of social relations and do not have the strength to react to changed situations in a new way. One can frequently find it in today's Europe, particularly in the German-speaking countries. It is in contrast to the emphatically optimistic and active discussion of how to shape a new world which goes on not only in America, but also in so-called Communist areas.

What, then, are the goals and possibilities for Europe in this world?

Stated briefly: the preservation, strengthening and securing of Europe by the only means now being made possible —namely, through global expansion and democratization of its dynamism, directed toward human goals in the framework of a vital policy embracing all of mankind. This vital policy should be aimed at the promotion of worldwide development and planning, whose scope must reach even beyond our planet. This means no more than drawing the conclusion from experience that there can be no more economic and cultural islands on earth, and that we have entered the stage of a worldwide neighborhood situation in which the development, welfare, indeed the survival of every member —whether individual or social group—is dependent on the possibility of the effective participation of all in the process and the fruits of development.

The impulses coming from Europe have so far been the strongest expansive forces in the history of mankind—in the positive as well as the negative sense. If Europe does not want to surrender itself, it has to continue to expand. If Europe does not want to continue mobilizing superior forces against itself, then this expansion must not be violent, one-sided and authoritarian, but peaceful, cooperative and carried out in the context of partnership.

On Learning the Last Displayed Role

In the past, Europeans have played a variety of roles in Asia, Africa and Latin America. They were conquerors, slave dealers and slave holders, exploiters, colonial rulers, but also missionaries, doctors, teachers, even peacemakers. In these roles they always acted the superior, and almost always as the infallible authority. Connected with this was usually another function, though mostly not desired and not understood: that of awakening the others to discontent, protest, even revolution. There is only one role which has not yet, or hardly ever, been played: the role of partner. To learn this role will be difficult for all those concerned on both sides. However, it must be learned. For partnership is the only role which is open for Europe in the future. Europe is small. Even a united Europe (within the frontiers set by the political possibilities) would be small in comparison to the other continents and major regions. Its contribution to the population of the earth is decreasing to an ever smaller minority. For Europe it is therefore of vital importance to promote a global society where territorial frontiers, racial differences and military strength play as unimportant a role as possible.

The relation of partnership means showing understanding for common goals and for the necessity of permanently working together at elastic, experimental planning to realize these goals, all the time remaining aware of the essential peculiarities of each partner. On the one hand, this implies that we must not expect our partners to adjust themselves to our ideological and political patterns. On the other hand, it means that there is no danger of Europe being simply integrated in a uniform global culture of the future or in a "European unity" where its different components would be "brought into line." . . . Certainly, European elements will be constant and universal ingredients of these mixtures. These will be most important, of course, in the Soviet Union, America and in the overseas territories settled by Europeans. At the same time, Europe will adopt more and more cultural elements from more and more non-European sources. Much of what we conceive of as being specifically European (and what is often no more than the local color of a static and traditionally authoritarian existence) is undoubtedly bound to die because its material and spiritual presuppositions no longer exist.

Pluralism as a Plus Factor

I do not believe that this also applies to the pluralism in the values and life styles gestated in Europe and in Europe alone in the last centuries—in contrast to the monism of all other and older cultures. It seems to me that this pluralism is not only capable of surviving, but that it is the necessary basis for the syncretism of the practical values—the values which we have already practiced within the Western tradition and which should now be applied to mankind in general. For this we have to learn, not only to tolerate others and their particularities, but also to appreciate them. All past cultures, the predynamic European culture included, were monistic and therefore one-sided, inelastic and easily threatened by changes of the natural or social environment. It is only now, in the modern European-American culture, that we have begun to appreciate pluralism positively—in-

stead of tolerating it at best as an unavoidable evil. Now
we all have to learn how to practice pluralism, together with
empathy and the strategy of cooperation, in the more complex and larger context of an intricate and unstable global
society. This will be the only way to acquire the social techniques of nonviolent settlement of conflicts which we must
have to create a peace embracing all of mankind—a peace
which cannot be based on angels and saints, but on people;
people, however, who show themselves highly capable of
learning.

Some men today advocate a policy of neutralism for all
European states in order to achieve military isolation from
world politics and thereby the condition for genuine European integration—also across the Elbe. But this view seems
to me inconsistent. The present disruption in the world will
disrupt Europe as well. Europe is still important enough to
cause the world powers to make allies here and to create and
maintain bulwarks. The only possibility for Europe to sur-
vive, to maintain its culture and eventually to unite—is to
work toward global peace by reducing the significance of
clashing ideologies, by introducing a matter-of-fact tone in
international relations and by adopting a policy of global
development. This policy of global development is particularly important, for otherwise there will be more and more
Vietnams and thus more occasions for worldwide conflicts.

One can already see a trend toward rapprochement in
the policies of the two postwar world powers, toward a peaceful order which will be more than a precarious balance of
terror. Until now this movement has taken place largely
without Europe's participation, even over its head . . . . It
seems to be in Europe's interest to become involved in these
efforts in order to avoid the role of a passive onlooker and
to take up a position of constructive participation backed
by its own, specific strength—lest it become an inert object.
This would be the only way to avoid a final split of Europe
into "West" and "East," a split which could even outlive
the acute tension between the two present world powers.

The more closed our ranks are as we march under a European banner, the more we think and act openly and pragmatically, the better will be our chance cautiously to move the European frontiers further to the East again.

Furthermore, it is necessary to resist the present strong temptation to think that in the new world situation Europe might be saved by regional integration—that is, by setting up walls around a quasi-self-sufficient "sphere of welfare" of the relatively developed peoples. To overcome the still-strong European nationalisms by creating an economically and politically united Europe . . . would require creating a new and geographically broader nationalist myth. Such a myth could only renew and increase the distance and tension between Europe and the outside world, the mistrust and resentment of those who have just emancipated themselves from dependence on Europe. Already, the European Economic Community has called forth a whole series of non-European attempts at integration, which is perfectly understandable but has led to irrational consequences in economic terms. We are simply about to perpetuate on a higher geographical level the collective egoism, with its good conscience and intellectual blinkers, so characteristic of nationalism. This can only make its consequences even more dangerous. A currently popular concept is that the way from nation to mankind must proceed gradually, beginning with the establishment of larger regional groupings. This view is unrealistic. It ignores the fact that the obstacles arising inside a continent are just as great as those within an open, more worldwide movement of integration. It also overlooks the fact that we no longer have time for the luxury of developing new restricted forms of action and the rivalries inevitably resulting from them. At present, all thinking and acting which is not oriented toward a global concept remains provincial—even if it is directed toward major regional dimensions.

BIBLIOGRAPHY

An asterisk (*) preceding a reference indicates that the article or a part of it has been reprinted in this book.

BOOKS, PAMPHLETS, AND DOCUMENTS

Amme, C. H. Jr. NATO without France. Stanford University, Hoover Institution on War, Revolution and Peace. Stanford, Calif. 94305. '67.

Ardagh, John. The new French revolution. Harper. '69.

Ball, G. W. The discipline of power: essentials of a modern world structure. Little. '68.

Barnet, R. J. and Raskin, M. G. After 20 years. Random House. '65.

Barzanti, Sergio. The underdeveloped areas within the Common Market. Princeton University Press. '65.

Baumann, C. E. ed. Western Europe: which path to integration? Heath. '67.

Beloff, Max. The future of British foreign policy. Taplinger. '69.

Brandt, Willy. A peace policy for Europe. Holt. '68.

Brinton, Crane. The Americans and the French. Harvard University Press. '68.

Bromberger, Merry and Bromberger, Serge. Jean Monnet and the United States of Europe. Coward-McCann. '69.

Buchan, A. F. ed. Europe's futures, Europe's choices: models of Western Europe in the 1970's. Columbia University Press (for the Institute for Strategic Studies). '69.

Calleo, D. P. Britain's future. Horizon. '69.

Calmann, John, ed. Western Europe: a handbook. Praeger. '67.

Catlin, George. The Atlantic commonwealth. Penguin. '69.

Caves, R. E. and others. Britain's economic prospects. Brookings. '68.

Center for Strategic and International Studies. NATO after Czechoslovakia. The Center. Georgetown University. 810 18th St. N.W. Washington, D.C. 20006. '69.

*Christoph, J. B. Britain at the crossroads. (Headline Series no 186) Foreign Policy Association. 345 E. 46th St. N.Y. 10017. '67.

Cleveland, H. van B. The Atlantic idea and its European rivals. McGraw. '66.

Dahrendorf, Ralf. Society and democracy in Germany. Doubleday. '69.

Deutsch, K. W. and others. France, Germany and the western alliance. Scribner. '67.

Djilas, Milovan. The unperfect society: beyond the new class. Harcourt. '69.

*Foreign Policy Association. Great decisions 1969. The Association. 345 E. 46th St. New York 10017. '69.
    Reprinted in this book: Fact Sheet no 1. Czechoslovakia, Russia and Eastern Europe. p 1-12; Fact Sheet no 5. Western Europe and the U.S.: western Europe at sixes and sevens. p 53-6.

*Foreign Policy Association. Great decisions 1970. The Association. 345 E. 46th St. New York 10017. '70.
    Reprinted in this book: Fact Sheet no 3. After de Gaulle, a new deal for France's allies? p 27-37.

Friedrich, C. J. Europe: an emergent nation? Harper. '70.

Gladwyn, H.M.G. Jebb, 1st Baron. Europe after de Gaulle. Taplinger. '69.

Grosser, Alfred. The Federal Republic of Germany. Praeger. '64.

Jaspers, Karl. The future of Germany. University of Chicago Press. '67.

Kesselman, Mark. France: the Gaullist era and after. (Headline Series no 194). Foreign Policy Association. 345 E. 46th St. New York 10017. '69.

Kissinger, H. A. The troubled partnership: a re-appraisal of the Atlantic alliance. Doubleday. '66.

Lichtheim, George. Marxism in modern France. Columbia University Press. '66.

Lichtheim, George. The new Europe: today, and tomorow. 2d ed. Praeger. '64.

Nicholson, Max. The system: the misgovernment of modern Britain. McGraw. '69.

Peccei, Aurelio. The chasm ahead. Macmillan. '69.

Pounds, N. J. G. and Kingsbury, R. C. An atlas of European affairs. Praeger. '64.

Sampson, Anthony. Anatomy of Europe. Harper. '68.

Servan-Schreiber, J. J. The American challenge. Atheneum. '68.

Spinelli, Altiero. The Eurocrats: conflict and crisis in the European community. Johns Hopkins Press. '66.

Steel, Ronald. Pax Americana. Viking. '67.

Zaring, J. L. Decision for Europe: the necessity of Britain's engagement. Johns Hopkins Press. '69.

PERIODICALS

Academy of Political Science Proceedings. 29:7-20. N. '68. NATO and the changing Russian threat. N. H. Wessell.

Academy of Political Science Proceedings. 29:36-48. N. '68. Britain and Europe. John MacGregor.

Academy of Political Science Proceedings. 29:80-94. N. '68. French nuclear deterrent. W. L. Kohl.

America. 119:100-3. Ag. 17, '68. Dreams and realities of Europe. J. V. Schall.

America. 120:556. My. 10, '69. World after General de Gaulle.

America. 121:27. Jl. 19, '69. New hope for European unity.

America. 121:349. O. 25, '69. Common Market showdown.

American Scholar. 37:94-110. Winter '67. Report from Paris: de Gaulle, which way to the future? Waverley Root.

*Atlantic. 221:12+. Je. '68. Report: Spain, struggle for post-Franco leadership. Loren Jenkins.

Atlantic. 224:14-16+. N. '69. France. Don Cook.

Atlantic Community Quarterly. 6:512-19. Winter '68-'69. The future of the Atlantic alliance. C. L. Patijn.

Atlantic Community Quarterly. 6:566-9. Winter '68-'69. Why Europe needs continental-scale firms. Guido, Colonna di Paliano.

Atlantic Community Quarterly. 7:18-38. Spring '69. What kind of Atlantic partnership. H. A. Kissinger.

Atlantic Community Quarterly. 7:39-47. Spring '69. I could not but feel a great anxiety. P. H. Spaak.

Atlantic Community Quarterly. 7:53-8. Spring '69. NATO: a new desire to exist. Carlyle Morgan.

Atlantic Community Quarterly. 7:315-20. Fall '69. The future of the Atlantic alliance. Robert Ellsworth.

Atlantic Community Quarterly. 7:321-33. Fall '69. The Atlantic alliance: institutional developments for the 1970s. Livingston Hartley.

Atlantic Community Quarterly. 7:378-86. Fall '69. Two views of France after de Gaulle. André Fontaine and Pierre Drouin.

*Atlantic Community Quarterly. 7:387-92. Fall '69. Aim: widened European community. George Brown.

Aviation Week & Space Technology. 89:21. N. 25, '68. NATO members move to bolster alliance. D. E. Fink.

Bulletin of the Atomic Scientists. 25:36-9. Ja. '69. Czechoslovakia and western security; statement. H. M. Jackson.

Bulletin of the Atomic Scientists. 25:10-14+. O. '69. Lack of scientific planning in Europe. J. Guéron.

Bulletin of the Atomic Scientists. 25:4-7. N. '69. France's new defense strategy and the Atlantic puzzle. M. J. Brenner.

Bulletin of the European Communities
        Monthly published by secretariat of the Commission of the European Communities, Brussels.

Business Week. p 93-4. Je. 29, '68. EEC reaches a momentous goal; uniform external tariffs.

*Business Week. p 53-6. N. 23, '68. Europe's merger boom thunders a lot louder.

*Business Week. p 128-30. My. 10, '69. Europe tries to keep its boom in balance; growth rates soar.

Business Week. p 88. Ag. 16, '69. France awaits the next storm.

Business Week. p 27. O. 4, '69. Winners inherit a heated economy.

*Business Week. p 112-14+. N. 1, '69. Germany's export boom steams right ahead.

Christian Science Monitor. p 1. Mr. 25, '69. Economic picture rosier: "twilight" dims European political unity. Carlyle Morgan.

Christian Science Monitor. p 1. Mr. 25, '69. Step by step: Brandt backs piecemeal approach to elusive goal of one Europe. H. B. Ellis.

*Christian Science Monitor. p 14. Mr. 29, '69. EEC makes headway on highways. H. G. Franks.

*Christian Science Monitor. p 12. Jl. 3, '69. Technology plus: joint European research develops cheaper A-plant. R. C. Cowen.

Christian Science Monitor. p 1+. D. 3. '69. Czech purge spreads alarm in East Europe. Eric Bourne.

Christian Science Monitor. p 4. D. 3, '69. Brandt urges prompt action to enlarge Common Market. Carlyle Morgan.

*Christian Science Monitor. p 1. D. 16, '69. Blueprint for unity in Europe. J. A. May.

Commentary. 45:48-53. My. '68. Europe and the United States. George Lichtheim.

Commonweal. 88:62-3. Ap. 5, '68. Spain tightens squeeze on intellectuals. Peter Steinfels.

Commonweal. 89:491-2. Ja. 17, '69. Crisis within a crisis. L. J. Berry.

Current History. 54:166-71+. Mr. '68. France and the Common Market crisis. P. H. Laurent.

Current History. 54:257-97+. My. '68. Report on West Germany; symposium.

Current History. 56:193-229+. Ap. '69. East Europe; symposium.

Current History. 57:42-7+. Jl. '69. U. S. and Europe today. S. D. Kertesz.

Department of State Bulletin. 58:392-7. Mr. 18, '68. German-American economic interdependence; address, January 15, 1968. G. C. McGhee.

Department of State Bulletin. 58:680-6. My. 27, '68. Europe and the United States, the partnership of necessity; address, May 3, 1968. E. V. Rostow.

Department of State Bulletin. 59:45-7. Jl. 8, '68. German eastern policy and reunification; address, June 17, 1968. G. C. McGhee.

Department of State Bulletin. 59:489-93. N. 11, '68. United States and Western Europe: the vital partnership; address, October 16, 1968. N. deB. Katzenbach.

Dissent. 16:426-30. S.-O. '69. Letter from Paris: between Pompidou and CP. Jean Bloch-Michel.

Economist. 229:18-19. N. 16, '68. Time to look forward.

Economist. 231:27+. Ap. 19, '69. Roots of violence.

Economist. 231:16-17. Ap. 26, '69. Hunting for growth.

Economist. 231:13-15. My. 3, '69. Adieu de Gaulle, adieu.

Economist. 231:13-15. My. 24, '69. One man's Europe.

Economist. 232:15-16. Jl. 5, '69. Politics, Italian style.

Economist. 232:16-18. Jl. 12, '69. Oh, moo.

Economist. 232:14-15. S. 13, '69. The opposition to Europe.

European Community
    Monthly published by the European Community Information Service, Washington, D.C.

Foreign Affairs. 46:476-86. Ap. '68. German policy towards the east. Willy Brandt.

Foreign Affairs. 46:503-18. Ap. '68. Where is Britain heading? R. V. Roosa.

Foreign Affairs. 46:562-74. Ap. '68. Italy: the fragile state. Luigi Barzini.

*Foreign Affairs. 47:251-65. Ja. '69. NATO after the invasion. Harlan Cleveland.

*Foreign Affairs. 47:697-710. Jl. '69. The Common Market after de Gaulle. H. van B. Cleveland.

Foreign Affairs. 48:39-50. O. '69. Realism in British foreign policy. Edward Heath.

Foreign Affairs. 48:80-96. O. '69. What forces for NATO? And from whom? A. C. Enthoven and K. W. Smith.

Fortune. 77:108-12+. F. '68. Second battle of Britain. Walter Guzzardi, Jr.

Fortune. 78:118. N. '68. Setbacks for the new Europe.

Fortune. 79:88-91+. Ap. '69. Germany catches its second wind. Philip Siekman.

International Affairs. 45:246-58. Ap. '69. Britain in Europe: historical perspective and contemporary reality. J. P. Mackintosh.

*International Herald Tribune. p 6. D. 15, '69. Poles eager to start talks with Bonn to normalize ties. C. M. Roberts.

*International Herald Tribune. p 7. Ja. 16, '70. European economy; a special report. Henry Giniger and others.

International Organization. 22:841-54. Autumn '68. United States and the European Economic Community: a problem of adjustment. H. C. Wallich.

Interplay. 3:14-16. Je-Jl. '69. The legacy of General de Gaulle. Denis Brogan.

*Interplay. 3:14-19. Ag.-S. '69. The making of Europe. R. F. Behrendt.

Journal of International Affairs. 22 no 1:1-120. '68. East-West detente: the European debate.

Life. 66:36. Ap. 25, '69. After twenty good years; an identity crisis for NATO.

Life. 67:33-4+. Ag. 8, '69. For Spain a royal restoration.

Look. 32:82+. N. 12, '68. United States and Europe after Vietnam. J. K. Javits.

National Review. 20:734+. Jl. 30, '68. Next phase of the Gaullist cycle.

National Review. 21:163-4. F. 25, '69. Crackdown in Spain.

National Review. 21:1061-2. O. 21, '69. Brandt and the bogeyman. W. S. Schlamm.

Nation's Business. 56:78-80+. F. '68. We must heal U.S.-Europe
rift. G. E. Bradley.

*Nation's Business. 57:20+. O. '69. Charting a course for the
North; foundations of Scandanavian common market. Felix
Morley.

NATO Letter
          Monthly publication of the NATO Information Service, Brussels.

New Leader. 52:6-8. My. 12, '69. A new French image. G. W.
Herald.

New Leader. 52:3-5. Jl. 7, '69. The challenge in France. G. W.
Herald.

New Leader. 52:15-16. N. 24, '69. Spain after Franco. Ray Alan.

New Republic. 159:19-21. D. 7, '68. Fate of Czechoslovakia. H. J.
Morgenthau.

New Republic. 160:16. Ja. 4, '69. European expectations. Philip
Ben.

New Republic. 160:17-19. Mr. 15, '69. Nixon's Europe in the new
era. John Osborne.

New Republic. 160:17-21. Ap. 5; 20-3. Ap. 12, '69. America and
France: minimum feasible misunderstanding. Stanley Hoffmann.

New Republic. 161:19-21. Jl. 12, '69. De Gaulle's legacy to Pompidou. Stanley Hoffmann.

New Republic. 161:21-4. Jl. 26, '69. How will France change?
Stanley Hoffmann.

New Republic. 161:12-13. O. 11, '69. Absent presence of General
de Gaulle. Philip Ben.

New Republic. 161:13-14. N. 15, '69. Harold Wilson's sound
pound. Anthony Howard.

New York Times. p 1+. Ap. 10, '69. NATO pondering course as
it enters third decade. Drew Middleton.

New York Times. p E 4. S. 21, '69. In France, Pompidou faces
critical economic tests. Henry Giniger.

New York Times. p E 2. O. 5, '69. Wilson talks a good game of
unity. Anthony Lewis.

New York Times. p E 3. O. 5, '69. Brandt gets his chance for the
promised changes. David Binder.

New York Times. p E 6. O. 19, '69. Pompidou is finding those de
Gaulle shoes hard to fill. Henry Giniger.

New York Times. p E 4. O. 26, '69. Brandt foresees "some tough moments." David Binder.

New York Times. p E 6. N. 2, '69. Storm over Brandt's policy toward east. David Binder.

New York Times. p E 6. N. 9, '69. Nato: quandary over Warsaw pact bid. Drew Middleton.

New York Times. p E 5. N. 30, '69. Market: courtship has ended in Britain. Anthony Lewis.

New York Times. p E 6. N. 30, '69. Germany: seeking new ties with old enemies. Paul Hofmann.

New York Times. p 6. D. 4, '69. Common Market of the 70's: European and U.S. views. C. H. Farnsworth and E. L. Dale, Jr.

New York Times. p E 5. D. 7, '69. Without de Gaulle it's a different market. Drew Middleton.

New York Times. p E. 7. D. 7, '69. Threat to Italy in conflict of extremes. R. C. Doty.

New York Times. p 5. F. 9, '70. Federalism gains in the Common Market. C. H. Farnsworth.

New York Times. p 3. F. 16, '70. Trade bloc is cheerful on outlook.

New York Times Magazine. p 32-3+. F. 18, '68. As Great Britain contracts to a mini-power, a wistful good-by to all that. James Morris.

New York Times Magazine. p 34-5+. My. 19, '68. Servan-Schreiber dreams big. Israel Shenker.

New York Times Magazine. p 23+. Mr. 9, '69. Spain is still afraid of itself. Richard Eder.

New York Times Magazine. p 36-7+. S. 7, '69. Behind the wall, the success story of Walter Ulbricht. J. H. Huizinga.

New York Times Magazine. p 34-5+. N. 30, '69. Willy Brandt's *wanderjahre* are finished. David Binder.

Newsweek. 71:42+. Je. 3, '68. France in chaos: is Gaullism dead?

Newsweek. 72:31-2+. Jl. 8, '68. Countdown is under way; prospects for post-Franco era. Arnaud de Borchgrave.

Newsweek. 72:40-1. Jl. 22, '68. Europe: the tarnished dream. Arnaud de Borchgrave.

Newsweek. 72:88. S. 23, '68. Business as usual? East-West business.

Newsweek. 72:52. N. 4, '68. Don Quixote lives; author calls for free elections.

Newsweek. 72:41. D. 9, '68. Is the balance changing in Europe?

Newsweek. 72:36-7. D. 23, '68. Chance for a new Europe. Arnaud de Borchgrave.

Newsweek. 73:17-19. Mr. 3, '69. Mr. Nixon goes to Europe.

Newsweek. 73:98. Mr. 17, '69. Alliance: United States and EEC countries. H. C. Wallich.

Newsweek. 73:48. Mr. 24, '69. Après moi. . . .

Newsweek. 73:44. Ap. 21, '69. Détente or delusion?

Newsweek. 73:48+. Ap. 28, '69. Dubcek falls and the Russians have their way.

Newsweek. 73:51+. Ap. 28, '69. Harold's hope.

Newsweek. 73:44+. My. 5, '69. Unquiet on the eastern front.

Newsweek. 73:41-2+. My. 12, '69. End of an era: France after de Gaulle.

Newsweek. 73:48-50. My. 12, '69. De Gaulle and his era.

Newsweek. 73:45. My. 19, '69. Europe after de Gaulle.

Newsweek. 73:47-8. Je. 2, '69. France: the making of a president.

Newsweek. 73:49-50. Je. 9, '69. France: and now the final vote.

Newsweek. 73:50-2. Je. 9, '69. Thinking big for Germany.

Newsweek. 73:42-3. Je. 23, '69. Enter President Pompidou.

Newsweek. 74:48+. Ag. 4, '69. Hard pill to swallow; Juan Carlos as next chief of state.

Newsweek. 74:41. Ag. 18, '69. No hope; minority government formed.

*Newsweek. 74:56+. S. 29, '69. Eurocracy and a new vision. Arnaud de Borchgrave.

*Newsweek. 74:33-4. D. 22, '69. Germany looks east: reshaping Europe.

OECD Observer
    Bimonthly published by the Organization for European Cooperation and Development, Paris.

Orbis. 11:996-1033. Winter '68. Future of the Warsaw pact. W. C. Clemens, Jr.

Orbis. 12:1098-136. Winter '69. West German foreign and defense policy. Elmer Plischke.

Orbis. 13:17-372. Spring '69. Special issue on NATO and European security.

Reader's Digest. 94:161-2+. Ap. '69. NATO: an alliance in search of a future. H. W. Baldwin.

Reader's Digest. 94:195-8+. Ap. '69. Il boom transforms Italy. Giovanni Agnelli.

Reporter. 38:22-4. Ja. 25, '68. Europe's lag in business skills; technological gap. R. E. Farrell.

*Saturday Review. 52:16-18. Mr. 8, '69. Toward a new partnership with Europe. G. C. McGhee.

Saturday Review. 52:25-7. Mr. 8, '69. Grand strategy of de Gaulle. S. K. Padover.

Saturday Review. 52:4. My. 24, '69. In the general's wake. Henry Brandon.

Saturday Review. 52:14-15. Ag. 16, '69. Europe in a time of change. Drew Middleton.

Senior Scholastic. 92:16. F. 29, '68. Economics and Europe.

Senior Scholastic. 94:11-12. My. 9, '69. Le grand Charles steps down; pursuit of grandeur.

Time. 92:18-19. N. 22, '68. NATO: in the wake of illusion.

*Time. 93:58-62. Ja. 17, '69. A society transformed by industry.

Time. 93:36. F. 28, '69. Uneasy lies the bloc.

Time. 93:24. My. 9, '69. Future of Franco-U.S. relations.

Time. 93:30. My. 9, '69. France enters a new era.

Time. 93:94+. My. 9, '69. Revolt of the little man; investors fear nationalization.

Time. 93:39-40. My. 16, '69. Challenger, front and center; candidates for de Gaulle's successor.

Time. 93:102. Je. 6, '69. Tensions of too much success.

Time. 93:35+. Jl. 25, '69. Clarifying the succession.

Time. 94:38. Jl. 25, '69. Seeking unity, slowly.

*Time. 94:43-4. D. 5, '69. The Common Market: burial or revival?

U.S. News & World Report. 64:21. F. 19, '68. Now, an end to Britain's special role as an ally.

U.S. News & World Report. 64:43-4. F. 26, '68. West Europe's changing future! U.S. reviews its policy as a dream fades.

U.S. News & World Report. 64:98-9. F. 26, '68. Italy strikes it rich.

U.S. News & World Report. 64:104-6+. Mr. 18, '68. Germany as a U.S. ally, a look at the future; interview. Klaus Mehnert.

U.S. News & World Report. 64:54-5. Je. 17, '68. When Europe looks ahead now.

U.S. News & World Report. 65:80-1. Ag. 26, '68. Fading dream of one Europe.

U.S. News & World Report. 65:27-9. D. 9, '68. Major crisis ahead in Europe?

U.S. News & World Report. 66:25-9. My. 12, '69. France after de Gaulle.

*U.S. News & World Report. 66:30-1. My. 12, '69. Future of Europe's boom; meaning to U.S.

U.S. News & World Report. 67:58-9. Ag. 25, '69. After devaluation and controls; another crisis for France?

U.S. News & World Report. 67:20+. O. 13, '69. Germany on a new path; which way will it lead?

Vital Speeches of the Day. 34:424-7. My. 1, '68. Perspective on the Atlantic alliance; address, March 23, 1968. H. M. Jackson.

Vital Speeches of the Day. 35:137-41. D. 15, '68. Italy, the United States and Europe; address, November 19, 1968. Egidio Ortona.

World Business (Chase Manhattan Bank). p 5-8. O. '69. The European Common Market: a progress report.